Rivers, Villag and Valley

Illustrated and hand scribed by Paul Snowdon

Based on an original idea from
Peter Rollins, Bath and North East Somerset Council

Follow the River Avon from Bristol City Centre to Bath ~ and on to Bradford-on-Avon. Then trace its main southern tributaries ~ the Wellow Brook to Norton Radstock and the River Chew to the Mendips -and you will encounter some of England's most historic countryside. A region of hills, lakes and green valleys scattered with unspoilt villages, sparkling rivers and a rich and diverse flora and fauna ~ yet remarkably this is also a region soaked in the story of mans engineering challenge - covering 5 millenia.

A statue of Isambard Kingdom Brunel, the famous engineer who built the Great Western Railway through North East Somerset.

Although this guide starts in Bristol its geographical focus is North East Somerset.

Avonmouth
Floating Harbour
Clifton Susp'sn Bridge
Welsh Back
Conham
Hanham
BRISTOL
Upton Cheyney
St. Catherine's
Bitton
Lansdown
Avon Cycleway
Swineford

Chapter 1: The Avon Valley

Chapter 2
Bath and the Limpley Stoke Valley

Keynsham
Dundry
Queen Charlton
Kelston
Bathampton
Batheaston
BATH
Bathford
Maes Knoll
Saltford
Corston

Chapter 4: The Chew Valley

Newton St Loe
Norton Malreward
Compton Dando
Claverton
Pensford
Englishcombe
Stanton Prior
Chew Magna
Stanton Drew
Dundas
Chew Stoke
Priston
Monkton Combe
Chew Valley Lake
Bishop Sutton
Combe Hay
Limpley Stoke

Chapter 3
The Valleys of the Wellow Brook

Wellow
Blagdon Lake
Ubley
Freshford
Compton Martin
Farleigh Hungerford
West Harptree
Midsomer Norton
East Harptree
Radstock
Norton St Philip

CHAPTER 1
THE AVON VALLEY

3D sketch of the Avon Valley between Bristol and Bath; the illustration represents the countryside covered in this chapter, although that which is beyond Bath falls within Chapter 2

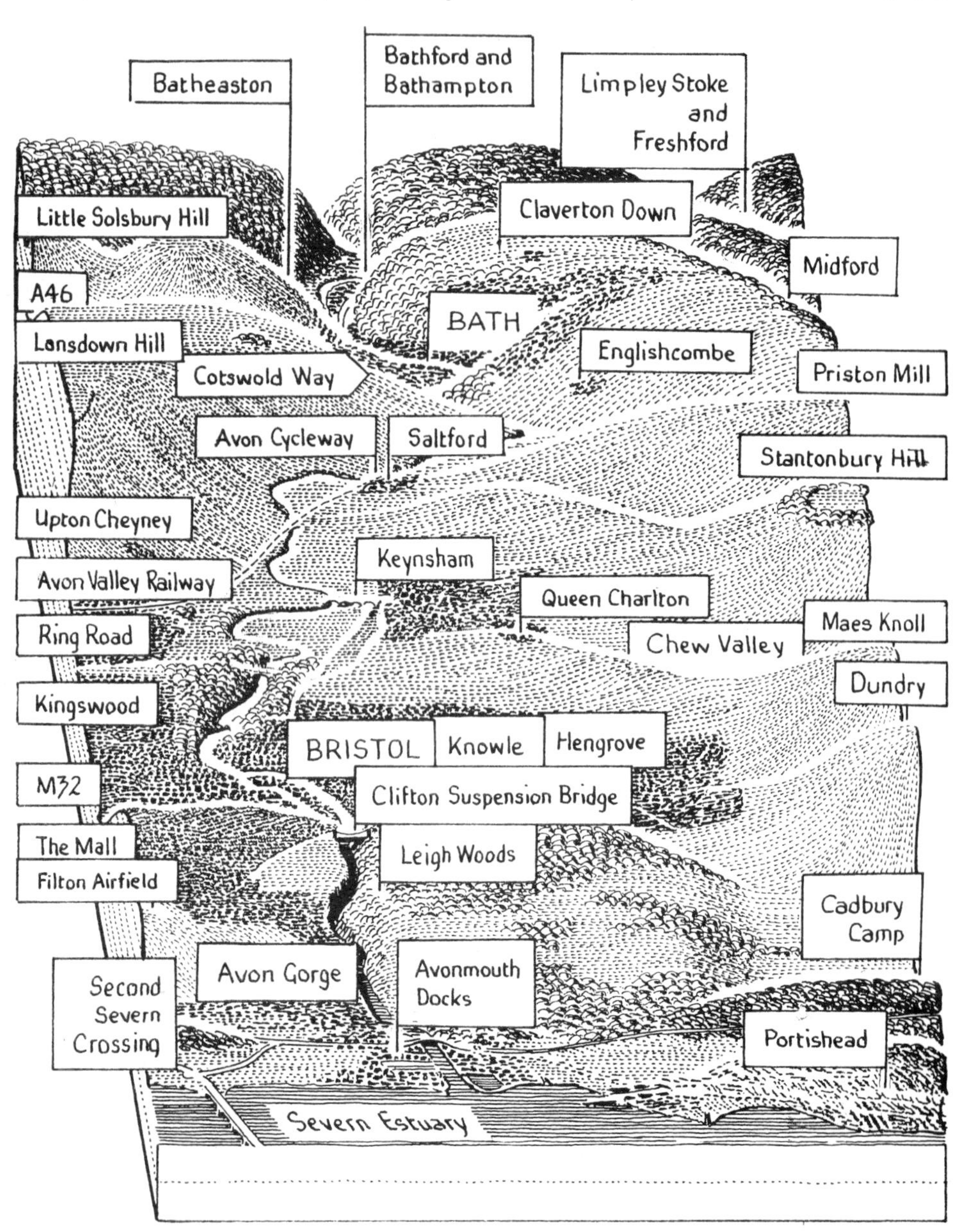

THE CHURCH OF ST MARY, REDCLIFFE

bears testimony to the Avon as one of England's greatest rivers.

But why is this Parish Church so grand? Often mistaken for Bristol Cathedral, it was described by Queen Elizabeth I as the 'fairest, goodliest and most famous Parish Church in England' even before the addition of its imposing 19th Century spire which rises 285ft above street level. The answer lies in the history of the River Avon, and in particular the Merchant Princes of 14th and 15th Century Bristol. Pioneering entrepreneurs, they established profitable European trade routes which brought wealth to Bristol, and enabled them to live ostentatiously on the riverbank. William Canynges was the richest of the local merchants, owning the largest fleet in Bristol, but after the death of his wife he renounced the world of commerce and entered the clergy, rebuilding St Mary Redcliffe and taking his first Mass in the new Church on Whit Sunday 1467. To this day, rushes are scattered on the Church floor every Whit Sunday to commemorate Williams ordination.

The River Avon was important as early as 1373 when Edward III not only granted Bristol a charter but made it a county in its own right; a just reward for trading dominance and the usefulness of Bristol ships in wartime. For the next 500 years Bristol ruled as Britain's second seaport, enjoying a renewed heyday from the 18th century increase in trade with America. Only in the 19th Century did the trade decline, passing to more accesible ports such as Liverpool, Glasgow and more latterly Avonmouth.

THE RIVER AVON

brought prosperity to Bristol from the east as well as the west. The stretch of river to Bath was opened for navigation in 1727 with the construction of seven huge locks: Netham Lock holds back the Avon's vicious 37ft tidal reach, after which Hanham, Keynsham, Swineford, Saltford, Kelston and Weston locks carry boats uphill towards Bath. In 1810 the great Kennet & Avon Canal saw its first traffic, connecting Bristol & Bath with the Thames to London.

The Parish Church of St Mary Redcliffe, Bristol

A PORT SIX MILES FROM THE SEA

It is Bristol's geographical position which first led to its emergence as England's second sea port. The navigable River Avon and the natural basin formed by its confluence with the River Frome form a defensible harbour, whilst its proximity to the great sheep wolds of the south west and Wales made it the natural exporting port for cloth. But Bristol is also a product of its great seafaring and enterprising people; the merchants who imported wine from Bordeaux and Spain, then after wars threatened their traditional links, ventured further afield to Iceland and, after the Cabots even to Newfoundland and the New World.

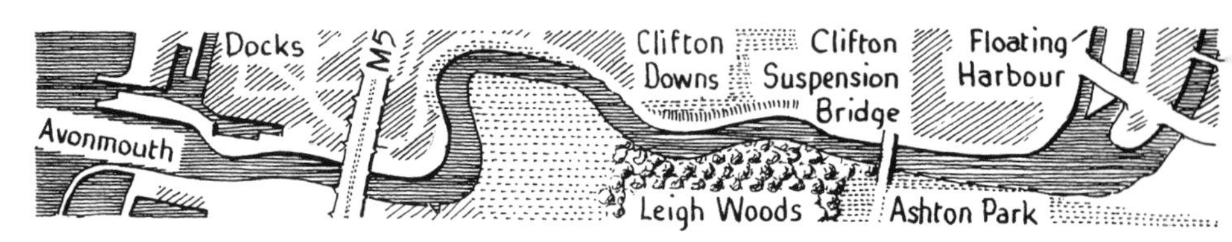

PIRATES, SMUGGLERS AND TREASURE ISLAND: The half timbered Llandoger Trow *(centre of the illustration below)* in King Street, built in 1664, became renowned as an 18th Century meeting place for pirates and smugglers; it's name comes from a type of Welsh coastal boat which frequented the busy Bristol harbour. The Llandoger Trow probably has strong literary connections too, for it may have been the "Spyglass Inn" in Robert Louis Stevenson's *Treasure Island*, in which case the Hispaniola of that book sailed from the nearby quayside on Welsh Back. It was probably also here that Daniel Defoe met the desert island castaway Alexander Selkirk whose true adventures were the basis of Robinson Crusoe

THE SS GREAT BRITAIN ploughs through an Atlantic storm *en route* to America, making history as the largest ship of her time *(3,443 tons burthen)*, the first to be built of iron and driven by a screw propellor. This ship was a product of Bristol, launched in 1843 and eventually salvaged from the Falkland Islands and returned to the Great Western Dry Dock of her birth 127 years later. Today, restored and resplendent she is open to view as a remarkable museum.

THE MARQUE OF BRISTOL shows a trading ship entering the City's great medieval castle, probably by its Watergate. Begun in the 12th Century as a motte-and-bailey, Robert Earl of Gloucester added a huge Caen-stone Keep which became a centre of power. Extended by Henry III and last used significantly by Edward I, the riverside castle has been skilfully excavated with explanatory signs on the site of what is now Castle Park in the City Centre.

A STATUE OF JOHN CABOT looks out over the Floating Harbour from the Arnolfini Centre. In 1496 John Cabot won funds from King Henry VII to explore new western sea routes to Asia. 1 year later he sailed from Bristol in the 50 ton "Matthew" to discover North America, giving the name "*New Founde Lands*" to the territory we know today as Newfoundland. In 1997, ~ the 500th anniversary of Cabot's voyage ~ a full sized replica of the Matthew sailed from Bristol to Bonavista, Newfoundland ~ the site of Cabot's original landfall. Today, the replica Matthew lies in the Floating Harbour, back in Bristol for all to see at close quarters. ~

BRISTOL'S FLOATING HARBOUR

CITY CENTRE SEASCAPE : a Sunday afternoon sketch of the many people who walk the wharves of the Floating Harbour, looking across towards Canon's Marsh and Brandon Hill.

THE UNUSUALLY NAMED "BRISTOL FLOATING HARBOUR" or "Float" as it used to be known is a unique City Centre waterfront where windsurfers and tall yachts rub gunwales with ocean going ships and narrow boats.

Begun in 1804, the Floating Harbour sought to make Bristol Docks "non-tidal". Its route through Bristol follows the original course of the River Avon, which was diverted along a new channel to the South - the "New Cut". Bristol Docks thrived until 1970 when their closure left the City with an unparalleled Civic water amenity.

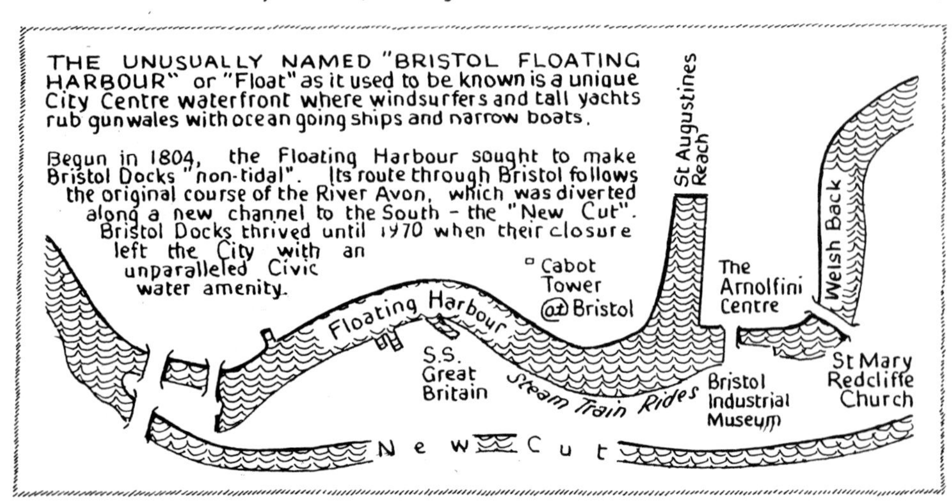

REGENERATION: A ferry passes the Watershed Media Centre in St Augustine's Reach, behind which @t Bristol creates another fascinating City Centre Venue.

TAKE A WATERFRONT RIDE in a steam train from the Bristol Industrial Museum on Princes Wharf; inside, the Museum explores Bristol's long association with transport.

ROYAL FOREST: Much of the area to the East of Bristol became known by the reign of Edward I as the Forest of Kingswood. Within its boundaries the King had absolute control, and as early as 1276 was selling licences to dig coal, thus starting a process of industrialisation through which most of the forest would disappear by the early 17th Cent. Within Kingswood however, are many ancient villages well worth a visit: the Upton Inn in Upton Cheyney *(illustrated)* appears almost still to be in the deepest Royal Woodland.

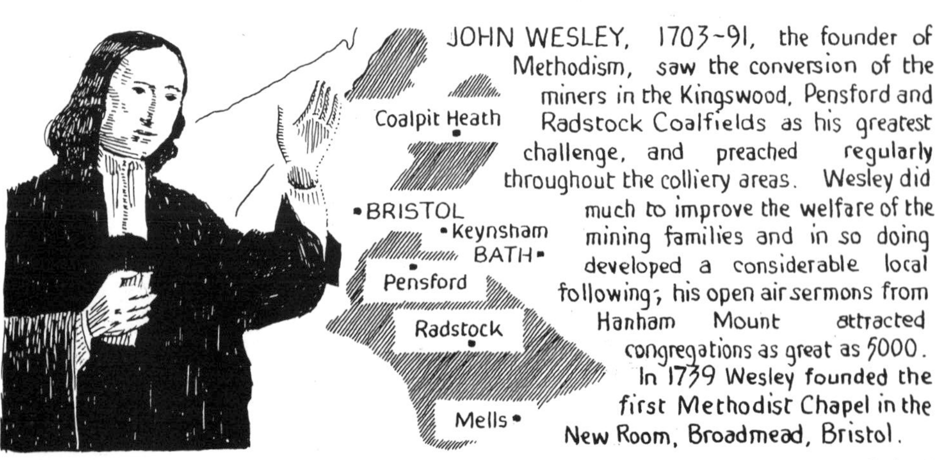

JOHN WESLEY, 1703~91, the founder of Methodism, saw the conversion of the miners in the Kingswood, Pensford and Radstock Coalfields as his greatest challenge, and preached regularly throughout the colliery areas. Wesley did much to improve the welfare of the mining families and in so doing developed a considerable local following; his open air sermons from Hanham Mount attracted congregations as great as 5000. In 1739 Wesley founded the first Methodist Chapel in the New Room, Broadmead, Bristol.

PREACHER TO THE COALFIELDS: John Wesley and the coalfields to the East of Bristol

LEAVING BRISTOL

Heading East along the Avon Valley, the excitement of a vibrant city soon gives way to the peace of open country.

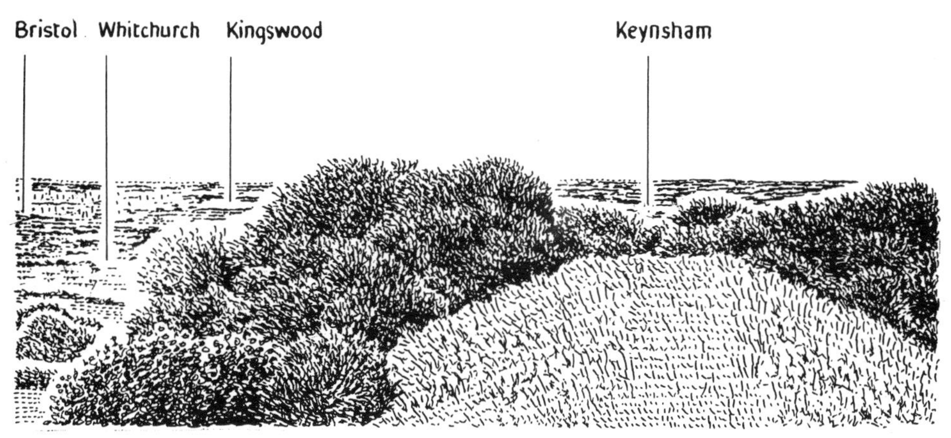

LOOKING NORTH: part of the view across the Avon Valley from the summit of Maes Knoll

Netham Lock holds back the massive 37ft tidal reach of the Severn Estuary; indeed the maritime expression "ship shape and Bristol fashion" derives from care needed to avoid damage from such a ferocious ebb tide. Once through Bristol's industrial zone the Avon cuts an attractive wooded valley, providing such retreats as the Conham River Park where a nature and history trail passes slag blocks from the former Conham Copperworks, the site of Conham Hall and the ford where persecuted Baptists were once chased out of Kingswood. The Avon Walkway forms a delightful riverside trail following the towpath.

ON THE FRINGE

The River Avon first meets North East Somerset at Hanham and then forms the boundary with South Gloucestershire until turning South at Swineford and entering N E Somerset more fully.

SWINEFORD PICNIC SITE was once an iron foundry, of which all that remains is the headrace and cascade; a number of pleasant footpaths lead away from the site, including an ascent of Lansdown Hill via North Stoke. The name Swineford derives from Prince Bladud, legendary founder of Bath and father of King Lear. Folklore tells that he forded the River Avon here with his swineherd before discovering the medicinal properties of Bath's hot water springs.

AVON VALLEY COUNTRY PARK is a riverside trail on which one encounters a range of rare and exotic species of animals and birds - from Vietnamese Pot Bellied Pigs to Bennet Wallabies - as well as Fallow Deer, sheep, goats, cattle, donkeys and Shetland ponies. Ponds and lakes provide boating and fishing, and, if they still have energy to spare, kids can also enjoy the assault course and play area.

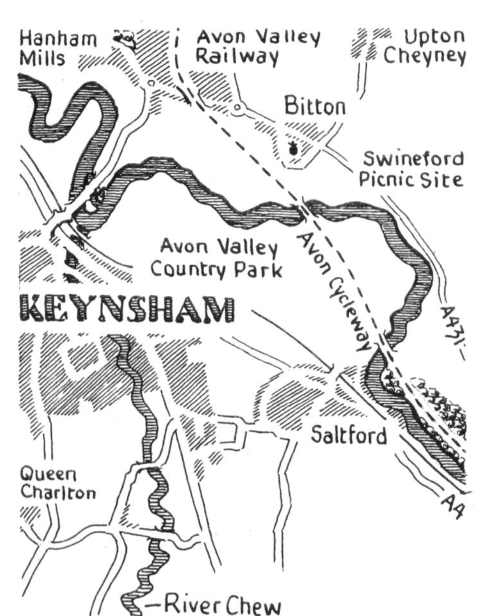

FROM RURAL TO ROYAL: Queen Charlton is the archetypal English village: attractive cottages, a Norman Church and a manor well spaced around a neat village green *(pictured)*. Although Queen Elizabeth I visited the village in 1574 to grant a charter for an annual fair, the "Queen" in its name is thought to come from Catherine Parr, the last wife of Henry VIII, who held Queen Charlton manor after the dissolution, and of whom evidence remains in the manor.

Catherine Parr

THE MAGIC OF STEAM returns to the Avon Valley at Bitton Station, thanks to a dedicated team of enthusiasts who have repaired the station, relaid the track to Oldland and organised both locomotives and rolling stock. The line was first opened by the Midland Railway Company in 1869 to connect Bath Green Park Station with the Bristol ~ Birmingham route. 97 years later, in 1966, passenger services were withdrawn and the track lifted in 1972. Today, as the picture suggests, the railway actively explores a wide variety of themes and activities!

RURAL RIVERSIDE PARADISE: yet Hanham Mills is just 5 miles from Bristol City Centre

KEYNSHAM

The rapid expansion of modern Keynsham has not detracted from the history of its ancient town centre.....

THE PARISH CHURCH OF ST JOHN THE BAPTIST *(illustrated above)* today dominates the busy Keynsham skyline. Its Somerset Gothic tower is a famous landmark, built in 1634 to replace a north transeptal tower which collapsed in a storm two years earlier. Much of the Church was restored in the 19th Century, but the lancets in the chancel are 13th Century, the pulpit 17th Century and the font is dated 1725.

THE ORIGINS OF KEYNSHAM are almost certainly Saxon, its Domesday Book name of *Canesham* probably originating from a tribal name. However, one of the more attractive, but less plausible stories told is that of St Keyna, beautiful daughter of Brychan, 5th Century Chief of Brechonshire. Fearing for her virginity, St Keyna fled her many suitors in her tribal home to seek refuge here, turning the many venomous snakes which infested the area to stone by the power of prayer. You can still see them in Keynsham today, coiled fossil sea shells called Ammonites *(see illustration, right)*. In fact the Ammonites were dug from local quarries, and some appear in the Church walls *(above)*

A fossilised Ammonite

RELIGIOUS DOMINANCE: whilst the Saxons built a minster in Keynsham whose Parish stretched as far as Publow and Chew Stoke, it was the Normans who really put Keynsham "on the map". In 1167 William, Earl of Gloucester, founded an Abbey here ~ one of six Augustinian monasteries in Britain *(all of which were in the West Country, with two others on the River Avon - Woodspring Priory and the predecessor of Bristol Cathedral ~ St Augustine's Abbey)* Keynsham Abbey was a great building whose tower rose high above the surrounding countryside; a settlement grew up around it which in 1307 was granted a market and an annual fair. By the 1530's the Abbey was sufficiently wealthy to own two fulling mills on the River Chew, but in 1539 dissolution by Henry VIII brought Keynsham Abbey to a sudden end and its great buildings were dismantled.

RUINS OF KEYNSHAM ABBEY in the town's Memorial Park

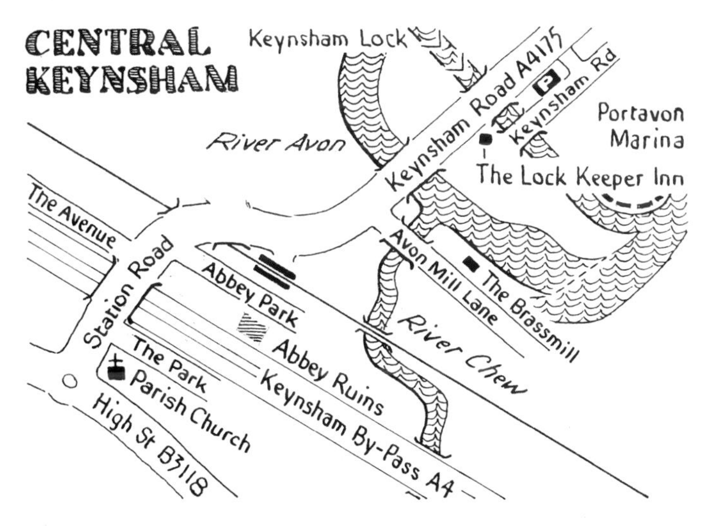

WATER POWER: The Brassmill ~ now a restaurant ~ connects Keynsham to the very beginnings of the Industrial Revolution. Abraham Darby opened 2 brass mills here in 1706 ~ one on the Avon and one on the Chew. Moving to Coalbrookdale (Shropshire) in 1709 he introduced coal to the smelting of iron which led directly to Britain's leadership in world iron production. Darby's son and grandson ~ both called Abraham ~ continued his work and in 1769 his grandson constructed the world's first iron bridge.

Darby's Keynsham mills were taken over by Nehemiah Champion; the Chew mill continued until the 1890's whilst the Avon Mill, working until 1927, produced brass plate for shells during World War One.

The Avon Valley

TALES FROM THE RIVERBANK

Walking the riverside path through Keynsham uncovers its rich local and natural history

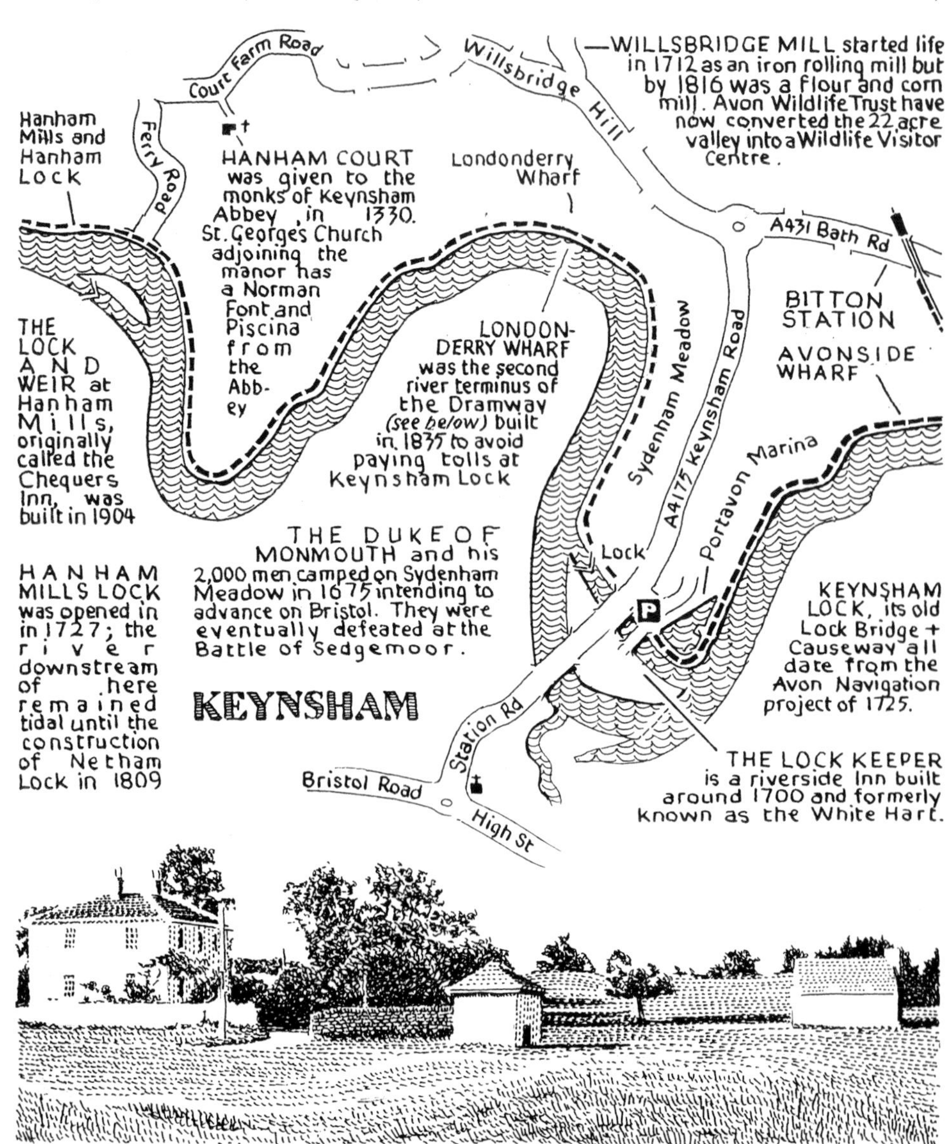

"WHERE ONCE STOOD A BUSY TERMINUS: Avonside Wharf near Keynsham was once a terminus for the Dramway – a track from Coalpit Heath laid to a gradient so that wagons laden with coal ran downhill to be unloaded into barges at the riverbank. Empty wagons were returned by horsepower. The alignment of track and sidings, the weighhouse, the blacksmiths stables and the carpenter's workshops can all be clearly seen.

TALES FROM THE KEYNSHAM RIVERBANK: Portavon Marina *above* overflows with boats whilst "The Lock Keeper" Inn serves riverside meals overlooking the weir. *Below*, Keynsham lock spills another group of boats downstream.

FIGHTING FOR THE HIGH GROUND-TO THE DEATH: the Monument to Sir Bevil Grenville commemorates his bravery in the Battle of Lansdown 1643 when Sir Bevil succesfully took and held Lansdown Hill for the Royalists in the English Civil War. The Monument marks the place where he was mortally wounded.

CAN YOU SEE FONTHILL? Beckford's Tower on Lansdown Hill was built in 1826 for the eccentric William Beckford. Having rebuilt Fonthill Abbey near Salisbury in 1807, he retired to Bath and built this tower in an attempt to see his beloved Fonthill from its top.

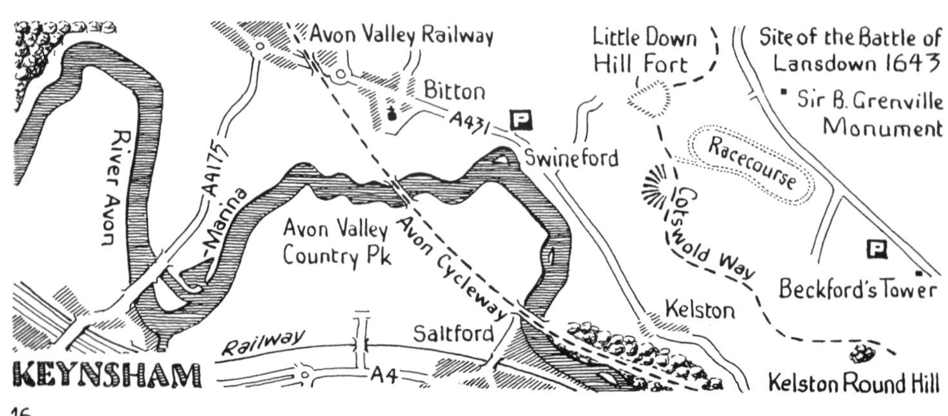

FIGHTING FOR THE HIGH GROUND

THE STEEP SIDED northern slope of the Avon Valley north of Saltford has enjoyed strategic importance in several phases of British history.....

AN IRON AGE WARRIOR *(600BC)* looks out across his promontory hillfort at Little Down towards the Avon Valley below. Iron Age soldiers built a line of spectacular hillforts along the Cotswold scarp, each with its ditch and rampart defenses still clearly visible.

Keynsham
Cadbury's Factory
Bitton Church
Bristol

...AND IF YOU CLIMB up to the Hillfort Ramparts the view back to Keynsham is rewarding

MESSING ABOUT ON THE RIVER

The meandering, tree lined River Avon between Keynsham and Bath offers facilities for a range of outdoor pursuits from sailing, rowing and cruising to cycling and riverside walking....

TRANQUILITY: local sailing clubs make good use of the River Avon near Saltford Lock

LOCKED INTO BATH: barges entering Bath on the River Avon rising within Weston Lock

LARGE ANNEALING OVENS mark the site of Kelston Brass Mill, built in the 1720's as a battery mill *(the process of shaping metal with a hammer)* powered by the flow of the River Avon. Behind the mill the Cotswold Scarp rises steeply towards Little Down Hillfort.

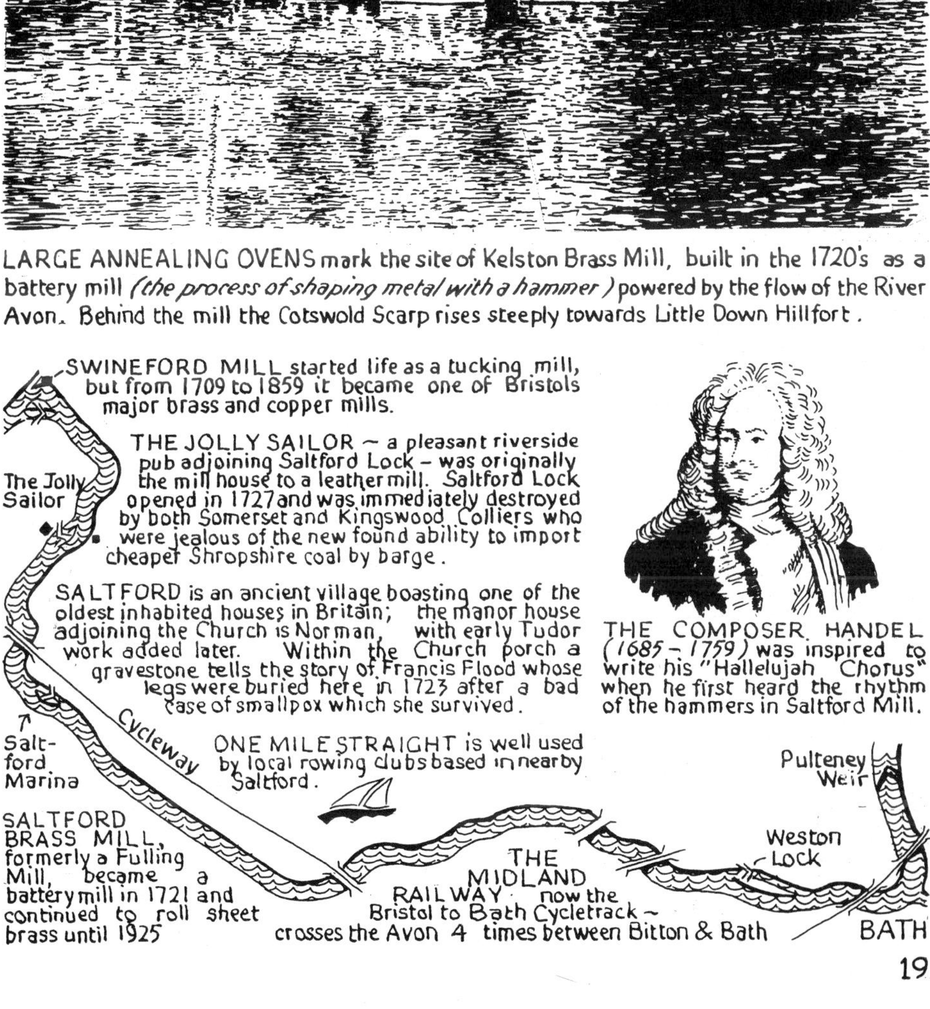

SWINEFORD MILL started life as a tucking mill, but from 1709 to 1859 it became one of Bristols major brass and copper mills.

THE JOLLY SAILOR ~ a pleasant riverside pub adjoining Saltford Lock – was originally the mill house to a leather mill. Saltford Lock opened in 1727 and was immediately destroyed by both Somerset and Kingswood Colliers who were jealous of the new found ability to import cheaper Shropshire coal by barge.

SALTFORD is an ancient village boasting one of the oldest inhabited houses in Britain; the manor house adjoining the Church is Norman, with early Tudor work added later. Within the Church porch a gravestone tells the story of Francis Flood whose legs were buried here in 1723 after a bad case of smallpox which she survived.

THE COMPOSER HANDEL *(1685 – 1759)* was inspired to write his "Hallelujah Chorus" when he first heard the rhythm of the hammers in Saltford Mill.

ONE MILE STRAIGHT is well used by local rowing clubs based in nearby Saltford.

SALTFORD BRASS MILL, formerly a Fulling Mill, became a battery mill in 1721 and continued to roll sheet brass until 1925

THE MIDLAND RAILWAY now the Bristol to Bath Cycletrack ~ crosses the Avon 4 times between Bitton & Bath

THE RIVERSIDE INN adjoining Saltford Marina overlooks Kelston Lock on the River Avon

FRENCH CONNECTION: Newton St Loe is one of the most picturesque villages in the Avon Valley: perfectly preserved by the Duchy of Cornwall it has a group of old stone houses, a 14th Century Church and a mansion. The name was given by the St Loe family, named in turn after St Lo in Normandy, who also owned the manor in neighbouring Corston.

The Avon Valley

SO CLOSE TO BATH, YET SO FAR

The gentle countryside to the south west of Bath is beautiful and timeless, a rolling rural landscape of rich meadows, well established hedges and mature trees. The area has been ignored by the main roads, still relying on an older web of *(very)* narrow lanes which predate the turnpiking of the through ways in the 18th century. Bath Turnpike Trust *(1707-1878)* encouraged traffic to follow the A39 to Marksbury and the A367 to Radstock, leaving the area in between as a sanctuary almost completely free from modern development.

WILD WILD WOODS: a slightly abstract picture of the ancient woodland nature reserve on Stantonbury Hill, which encloses another Iron Age Hill Fort. The Wansdyke *(see next page)* connects this prehistoric site with Englishcombe, Maes Knoll and Compton Dando.

STANTON PRIOR is an idyllic stone built village which used to belong to the Priory at Bath until the dissolution. Indeed the arms of Bath Abbey can still be seen in the 13th Century Parish Church of St Lawrence.

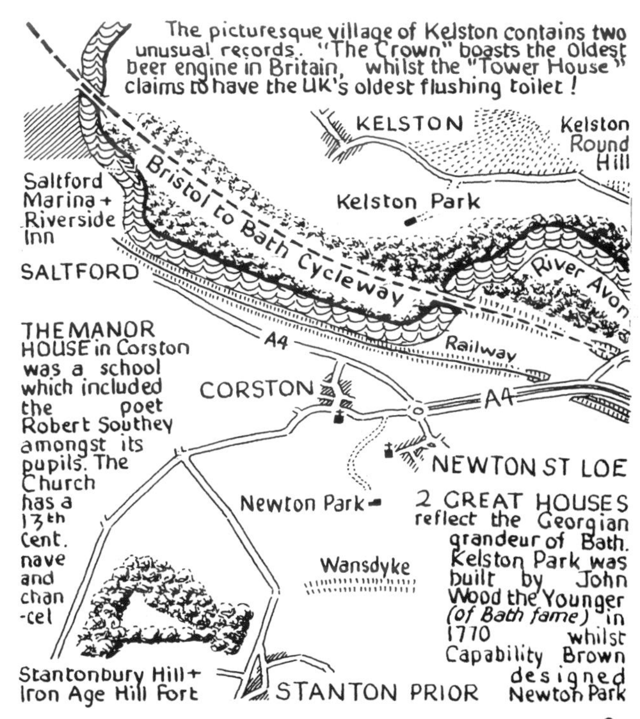

PRISTON MILL

HISTORY COMES TO LIFE at Priston Mill where the Conygre Brook drives a 21ft diameter Pitchback Waterwheel *(illustrated left)* which in turn powers the millstones making stone ground flour for bread. Continuing a tradition which started 900 years ago the whole process is open to public view, after which one can buy the flour in the little gift shop.

AND AFTER VISITING THE MILL explore Priston Mill Farm in true agricultural style

THE CONYGRE BROOK

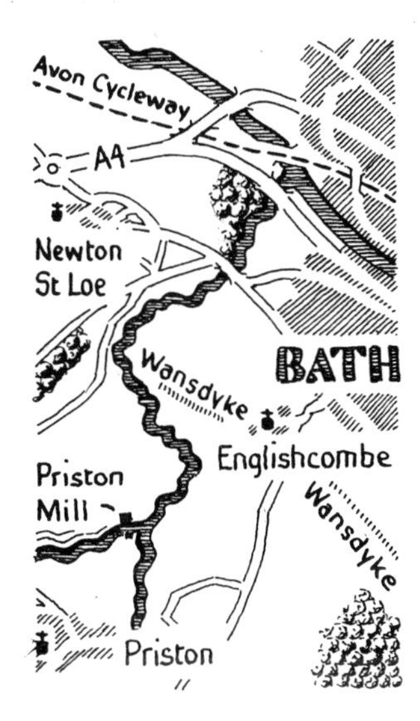

PRISTON is a quaint little village whose Church has a Norman nave and a central tower of 1751 which is somewhat dwarfed by its enormous weathercock *(see illustration, right, the drawing of which gave me a stiff neck!)* Folklore surrounds the origins of this oversized weathercock: one story tells that the weathercock was ordered for one of the "tallest Church towers in England" – a statement some distance from the truth! Another tells that it was erected in 1813 by the Lord of the Manor and inflated to satisfy his pride.

DWARFED! Priston Church

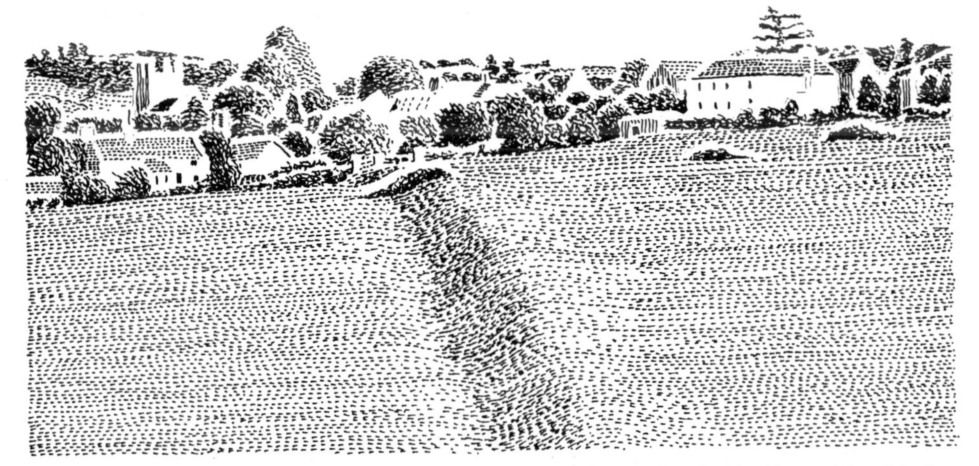

A VIEW OF ENGLISHCOMBE across the Conygre Brook, with the Wansdyke in the foreground. This great boundary bank was built by the ancient Britons in the 6th and 7th Centuries AD in an attempt to arrest the advance of the invading Saxons. "Woden's Dyke" as the Saxons called it stretched from Bristol to the Wiltshire Downs and its ramparts are still apparent in fields close to the villages on its route - Englishcombe, Compton Dando, Stanton Prior and Marksbury. Close to Englishcombe Parish Church a mound is all that remains of Culverhay Castle - a motte-and-bailey once the manorial seat of the Gournay family; in 1327 Thomas de Gournay was implicated in the murder of King Edward II at Berkeley Castle.

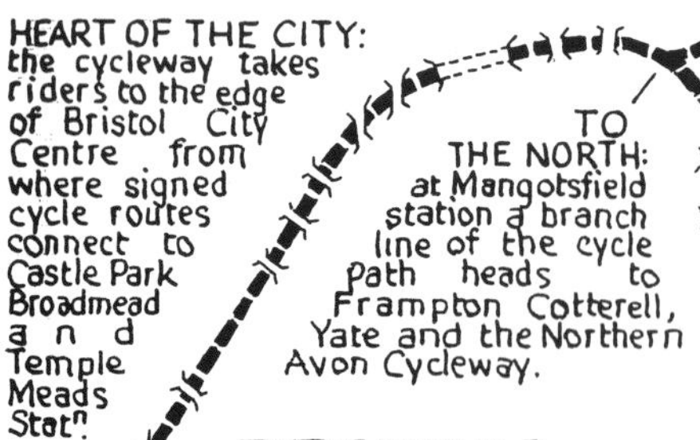

The Bristol and Bath Railway Path was completed in 1986 as a "permissive off highway route" for cyclists, pedestrians and wheelchair users. Connecting Bath and Bristol City Centres the path largely uses old railway tracks to give gradients which are pleasantly gentle for novice cyclists! Memorabilia from the age of steam abounds: bridges stations and the 470 metre Staple Hill Tunnel are all brought into context by the restored and "in steam" Avon Valley Railway at Bitton. Cyclepath and railway run parallel here for several miles, and refreshments are available at Bitton Station for those in need.

Avon Valley Railway at Bitton

PLAYING WITH THE RIVER: the cyclepath intertwines with the River Avon as it approaches Bath, crossing it 4 times on massive 19th Century iron railway bridges.

Saltford

RIVERSIDE CYCLING: the cyclepath enters Bath along the banks of the River Avon

BATH

A circular 80 mile route, the A

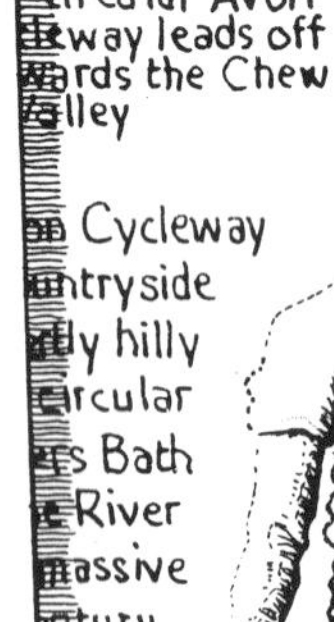

along the line of the Avon Cycleway,

CYCLING ON OLD RAILWAY TRACKS

A DOUBLE HEAD OF STEAM pulls the "Pines Express" out of Bath Green Park Station en route to Bournemouth, building up speed ready to climb the steep "1 in 50" incline up to Combe Down. Until its closure in 1964 the Somerset and Dorset Joint Railway became the most characterful of all Englands cross country lines, running through charming countryside and climbing to an almost alpine - *in train terms* - 811 feet at Maesbury Summit. The first stops were Midford (after 11 mins), Wellow (17 mins), Shoscombe (21 mins), Radstock North (28 mins) and Midsomer Norton South (36 mins). But Bath Green Park Station was originally opened by the Midland Railway in 1869 to link Bath with Mangotsfield and Bristol; it is this line which in 1986 reopened as the "Bristol and Bath Railway Path". Bath Green Park Station has been superbly restored and now forms part of Sainsbury's and the Farmer's Market.

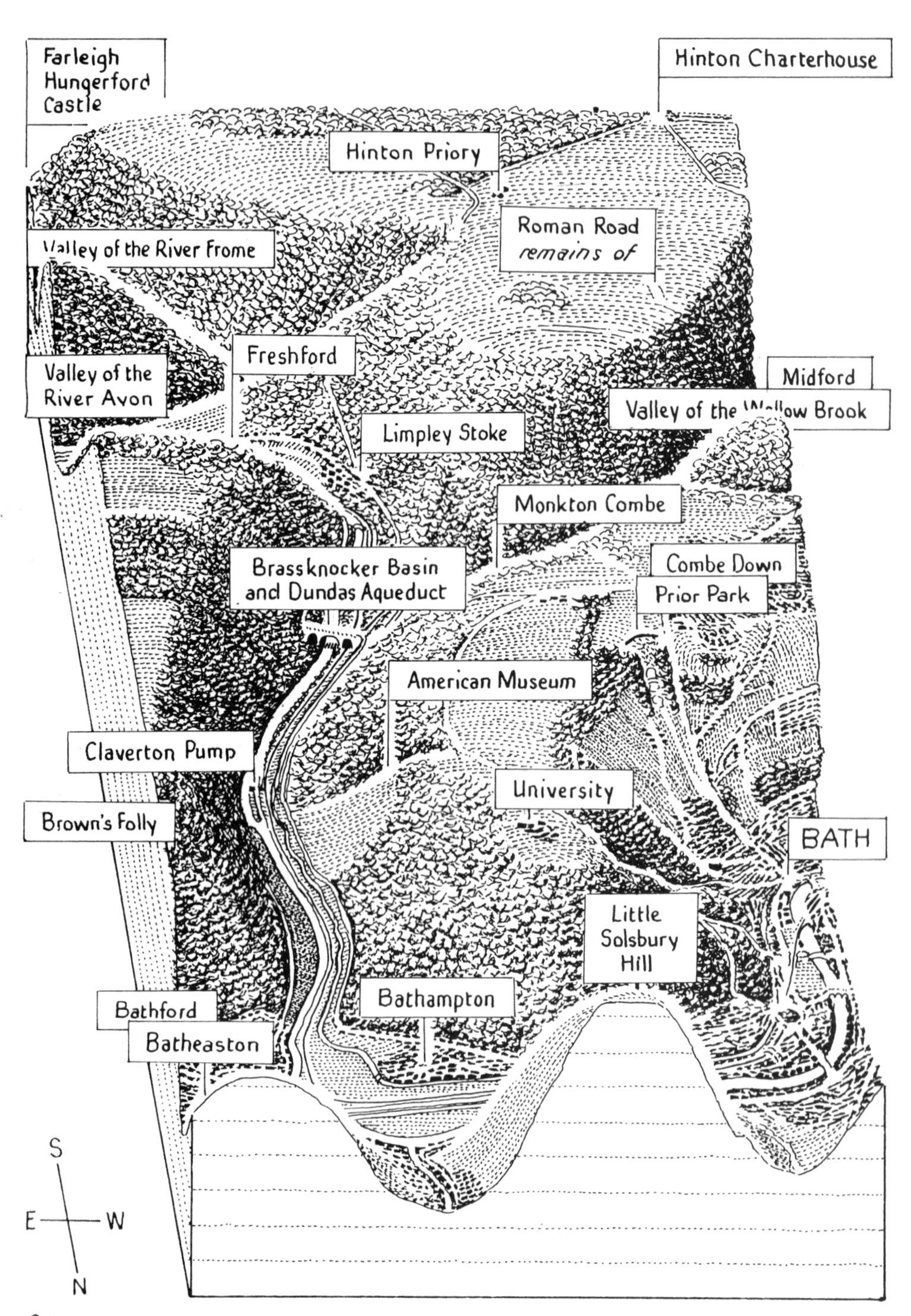
Farleigh Hungerford Castle
Hinton Charterhouse
Hinton Priory
Roman Road remains of
Valley of the River Frome
Freshford
Valley of the River Avon
Midford
Valley of the Wellow Brook
Limpley Stoke
Monkton Combe
Brassknocker Basin and Dundas Aqueduct
Combe Down
Prior Park
American Museum
Claverton Pump
University
Brown's Folly
BATH
Little Solsbury Hill
Bathampton
Bathford
Batheaston
S
E
W
N

CHAPTER 2

BATH AND THE LIMPLEY STOKE VALLEY

FIRST SIGHT OF PULTENEY BRIDGE as one enters Bath by boat along the River Avon. The bridge we are about to pass under is North Parade whilst the moorings on the right give good access to the City Centre with its wealth of characterful shops.

BATH needs little introduction as a world heritage site which exudes culture and history. From the Roman Baths where excavations and restoration provide an extraordinarily vivid picture of life 2,000 years ago, to the breathtaking view of Royal Crescent ~ a Georgian architectural creation unmatched anywhere in Europe.

As the '3D aerial view' *on the opposite page* shows, the River Avon meanders through Bath towards Bathampton from where it turns sharply to the South to carve the Limpley Stoke Valley. Peace and tranquility create a seductive beauty in this steep sided, wooded vale, made all the more attractive by its rich transport heritage. For the railway and the K & A Canal crowd in here too, reaching a climax at the mighty Dundas Aqueduct.

BATH

BATH SKYLINE the famous view across the rooftops towards Kelston Round Hill *(see page 21)* and Lansdown *(page 16)*. The line of trees in the foreground marks the route of the River...

WOODEN SKIFFS PUNTS AND CANOES awaiting hire at Bath Boating Station – a living museum of Victorian tradition offering tuition for inexperienced punters

A HUGE PORTICO OF GIANT CORINTHIAN COLUMNS dominates the front of Prior Park House, built in 1735 by Ralph Allen *(see page 34)*. Having amassed a fortune from his postal and quarrying enterprises, Allen bought this parkland - originally owned by the Priors of Bath Abbey - and commissioned John Wood the Elder *(see page 33)* to design a full blown Palladian mansion. From the North front - *illustrated* - a grandiose stairway leads out to Prior Park Landscape Garden which Allen created with help … Lancelot "Capability" Brown. Restored by the National Trust, the ga… ow open but as there is no parking nearby, visitors … garden are encouraged to use public transport

AN ORNAMENTAL BRIDGE crosses the fishponds in Prior Park. Built in 1735 it was based on the bridge crossing the Nadder at Wilton House and today boasts graffiti from the 18th century !

Bath and the Limpley Stoke Valley

THE KENNET AND AVON CANAL

One of Britain's most important canals starts *(or finishes, depending on your direction of travel)* in Bath then snakes its way eastwards literally clinging to the edge of the Limpley Stoke Valley. Whether you are navigating in a barge or walking the towpath the canal's passage through Bath forms a treasure trove of canal memorabilia, with iron bridges, two ornate pumping station chimney stacks, a lock keeper's cottage, stables for the horses which pulled the barges, a maltsters and a plethora of rope worn iron and stone work.

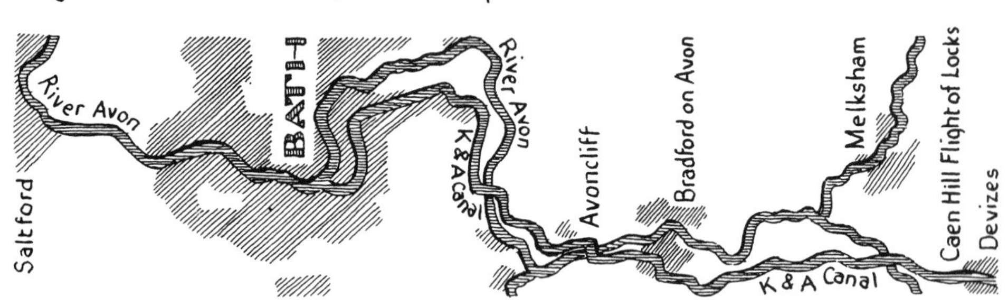

CLEVELAND HOUSE was built by Henry, Duke of Cleveland, in 1825 and became the headquarters of the Kennet and Avon Canal Company. It sits over the Southern Sydney Park tunnel and a hole which still exists in the tunnel roof was used to pass invoices to the barges below!

PUSHING WATER UPHILL: an incredible flight of 6 locks lifts the Kennet and Avon Canal 60 ft up the side of the Avon Valley within the first mile of its length *(locks 1-6 are on the R. Avon)*

60 feet

Lock 7

Locks 8/9

Lock 10

Lock 11

Lock 12

Lock 13

Follys Bridge

Candys Bridge

SYDNEY GARDENS: two short tunnels guard the canal's passage through the almost secret world of Sydney Gardens, where the canal is spanned by two wrought iron bridges.

SYDNEY WHARF was once the commercial heart of Bath's thriving canal trade; At its peak ~ in 1838 ~ the canal handled 341,000 tonnes of freight

Lock 13

Lock 12

Lock 11 Widcombe Locks

Lock 10

Locks 8/9: the awesome combination of locks 8/9 caused by the construction of a new road gave Bath Deep Lock - England's deepest canal lock; water rise 19 ft.

BATH

River Avon

Lock 7

PARTING OF THE WATERS: the Canal leaves the River Avon at Widcombe Lock *(illustrated above)*. Thimble Mill, beside the lock, was built as a pumping station to reclaim lock-fulls of lost water back in to the canal, and is now a hotel and restaurant.

THE KENNET AND AVON CANAL opened in 1810 to provide a wide beam passage from the River Avon at Bath to the River Thames at Newbury. 86½ miles of canal and 105 locks enabled barges up to 73ft long and drawing up to 3ft 6ins to sail from the West coast of England to the east, connecting the two great ports of London and Bristol

The canals useful life, however, was short: the Railway Age followed close on the heels of the Canal Age and in 1841 the first train provided a more attractive connection between Bristol and the East. Such was the resultant loss of trade on the canal that in 1852 it was sold to its main competitor ~ the Great Western Railway - for £210,000. Under its new owners little was done to encourage either commercial or pleasure traffic with the result that for much of the 20th Century the Kennet and Avon Canal was navigable only with difficulty. The last through passage from end to end was achieved in 1951. The canal closed.

A MAGNIFICENT VIEW of Bath awaits walkers + bargees from this area.

HAMPTON QUARRY WHARF: Hampton Quarry - on the Downs above the canal ~ furnished much of the stone used on the canal. It was brought down the hill by tramroad ~ which is still traceable

WROUGHT IRON BRIDGES in Sydney Gardens, Bath

Attempts to abandon the K & A were, however, thwarted and restoration soon started. In 1990, the Kennet and Avon Canal re-opened and is today enjoying a second heyday. But instead of freight it now carries people!

Bath and the Limpley Stoke Valley

THE BATH TRIO

A postman's nightmare! Follow the River Avon and the canal East out of Bath and the next three villages are Batheaston, Bathford and Bathampton. *For map please see next page*.

BATHFORD TO BATHEASTON: the view from Bathford across the Avon Valley towards Batheaston and Little Solsbury Hill, crowned by one of England's oldest Iron Age Hill Forts.

CANALSIDE REFRESHMENTS: the George Inn at Bathampton dates back to the 17th Century

PISTOLS AT DAWN: the mortally wounded loser of Britain's last legal duel was brought to the George Inn in the late 18th Century. Viscount du Barry, nephew of Louis XV's mistress, quarrelled with his friend Colonel Rice on Bathampton Down and is now said to haunt the Inn.

WINGS OUTSTRETCHED ~ a large stone eagle perches on the gable of Eagle House *(illustrated left)* built in 1725 by John Wood the Elder ~ founding father of Bath's Georgian reconstruction. Eagle House is in Northend, the oldest part of Batheaston, from where a beautiful valley winds up to St Catherines Court. Arguably Britain's most beautiful Tudor house, its 12th Century chapel is illustrated above *(right)*.

MEMORIES OF AUSTRALIA: The first Governor of New South Wales ~ Admiral Arthur Phillip ~ is buried in Bathampton Church *(illustrated above)*. As a naval officer Arthur Phillip organised the first western colonisation of the subcontinent, escorting the first shipload of convicts, selecting the site for the first settlement and naming it after the Home Secretary who originated the idea of a penal colony ~ Sydney. His grave was obscure until 1891 when Australian authorities traced his burial place to Bathampton; then in 1967 an existing chapel within the Church was converted into the "Australian Chapel".

CLAVERTON MANOR was built in 1820 by Sir Jeffrey Wyattville who also renovated Windsor Castle for King George IV. It now houses the American Museum in which the rooms and gardens relive scenes from periods of American history. In this manor on 26 July 1897 Winston Churchill made his first political spech.

VOLUNTEERS lovingly restore the Claverton Pump, built to maintain the level in the K & A Canal by pumping water from the River Avon below. Open at weekends.

PHILATELY GETS YOU EVERYWHERE: Ralph Allen's mausoleum is in Claverton Churchyard. As Bath's assistant postmaster in 1710 Allen made his fortune developing a cross country postal system. But it was his zealous belief in the quality of Bath stone which inspired the development of Georgian Bath from 1728 to 1830.

CLAVERTON

THE "CLOVER FARM" which belonged in the middle ages to the Bishops of Bath and Wells is now a small but attractive village bypassed by the busy A36. Claverton saw action in the English Civil War; one Royalist and three Parliamentary soldiers were killed by the river ferry and are buried by the West wall of the churchyard.

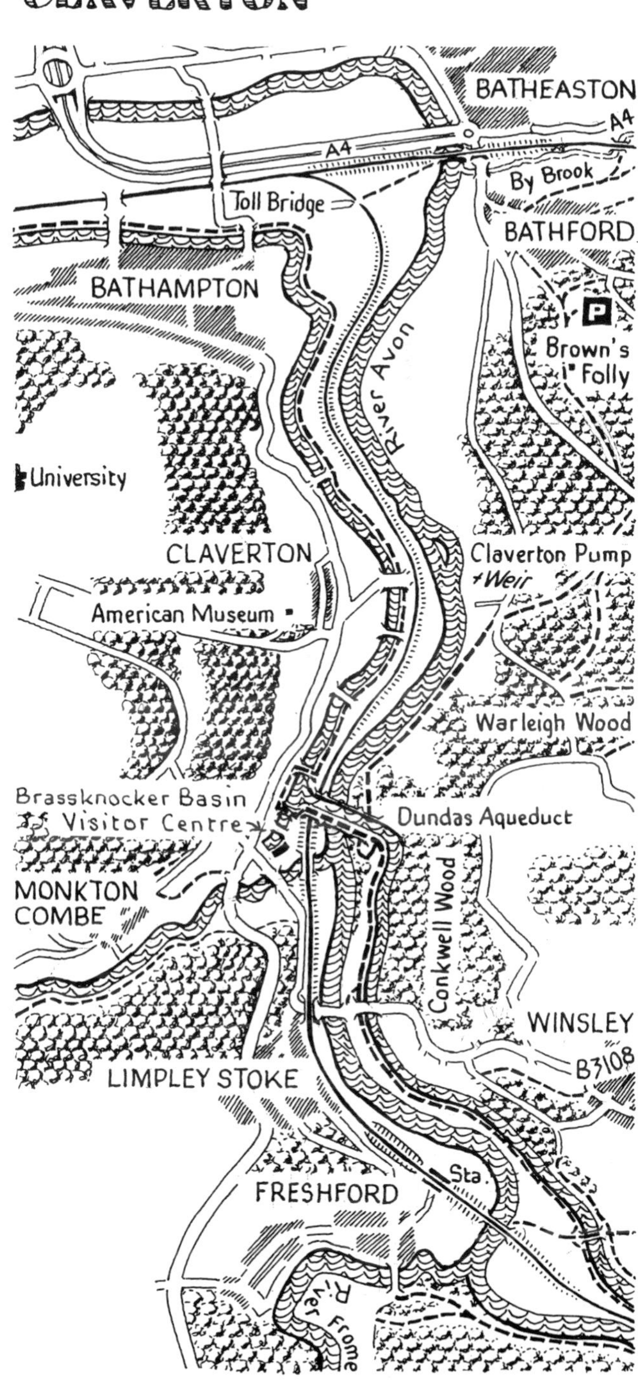

GOOD DEED: Mr Wade Brown commissioned "Brown's Folly" to provide employment for local labour after the Napoleonic Wars. Today the mature woodland over which it towers is a nature reserve.

THE NEWEST ATTRACTION ON THE CANAL is a Visitor Centre in Brassknocker Basin. Here a cafe, gift shop, museum, information centre and bookshop combine with an activity centre where cycles and boats can be hired....... and if you find your day afloat enjoyable you can even buy your very own barge here! *For location please see previous page.*

THE SOMERSETSHIRE COAL CANAL: Technically speaking, Brassknocker Basin is not on the Kennet and Avon Canal but on a short spur which once formed the start of the Somersetshire Coal Canal. In the late 18th Century the Somerset collieries were keen to gain access to the wider markets which the K & A offered, so built a canal connecting Limpley Stoke with Paulton and Timsbury; at Midford a second arm headed off towards Radstock via Wellow. Initial success was followed by failure to compete with the GWR, to whom the canal was sold in 1904 and who then built the Camerton to Limpley Stoke Railway over much of the canal's course. This railway itself then closed in 1951, enjoying a brief respite in 1953 when it was used to film *the Titfield Thunderbolt*

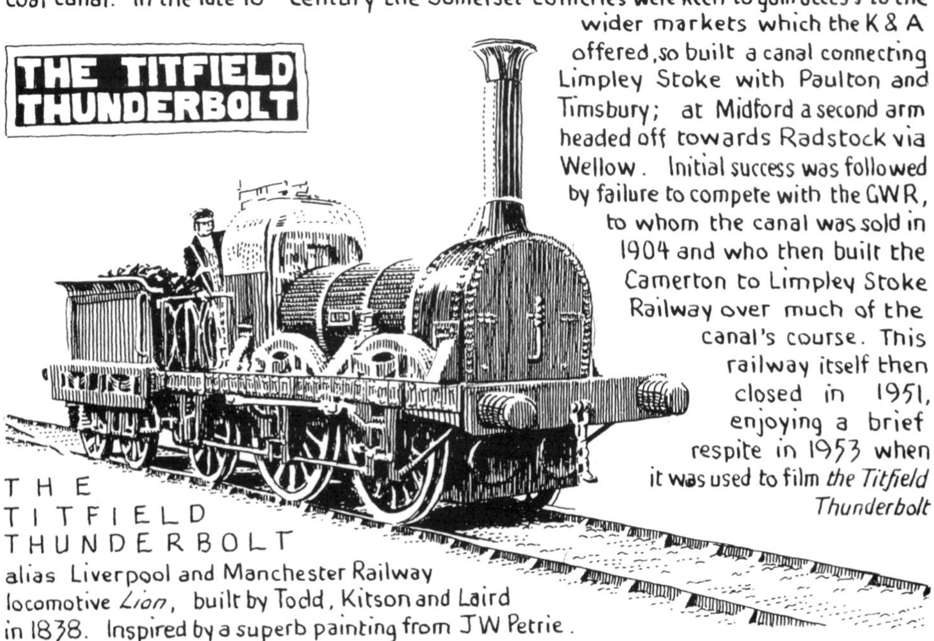

THE TITFIELD THUNDERBOLT
alias Liverpool and Manchester Railway locomotive *Lion*, built by Todd, Kitson and Laird in 1838. Inspired by a superb painting from J W Petrie.

IMPRESSIVE CANAL ENGINEERING

DUNDAS WHARF, BRASSKNOCKER BASIN AND THE GREAT DUNDAS AQUEDUCT, all grouped together near the A36 close to Limpley Stoke, have become the focal point of the Kennet and Avon Canal. Here too is the start of one of Britain's most successful – in its time – and technically challenging canals: the Somersetshire Coal Canal once carried over 100,000 tonnes of coal a year from collieries in Paulton Timsbury and Radstock to meet the K.& A. at Limpley Stoke. *(Map on previous page).*

CLASSICAL CURVES: The mighty Dundas Aqueduct carries the Kennet and Avon Canal across the River Avon, forming one of England's most dramatic bridges. Designed by John Rennie *(1761-1821)* in 1804 it was built from Bath Stone quarried in the adjoining Conkwell Wood. Rennie borrowed lavishly from the Georgian style of Bath: doric columns stand between one wide central arch and two upright side arches, supporting a beautifully decorated cornice.

FROM ABOVE: Dundas Aqueduct could easily pass unnoticed, appearing merely as a narrowing of the canal. This illustration is drawn from Dundas Wharf, on which sit a variety of original canal artefacts: a stone warehouse, iron crane, toll office and a grooved post.

...AND ON TO BRADFORD-ON-AVON

River and canal run parallel into Bradford-on-Avon, or *Broadford-on-the-River* ~ as the Saxons called it. Eventually the ford was replaced by a bridge and the drawing *(left)* shows two arches of the original 13th Century bridge remaining as part of a larger structure. The bridge chapel became in due course the town lock up in which the bed-steads can still be seen clamped to its interior walls. Overhead the impressive weathervane bears a symbolic fish - the Bradford Gudgeon.

Bradford is a town of great history; in October 1794 the first sod of the K & A Canal was cut here. Its Saxon Church was rediscovered in 1856 after being hidden for centuries and is probably the oldest place of Christian Worship in England. Bradford's famous 14th Century Tithe Barn was once used to collect payment in kind or "Tithes" for the great Abbey in Shaftesbury, whilst the Parish Church of Holy Trinity is 12th century with additions and 19th Century restoration.

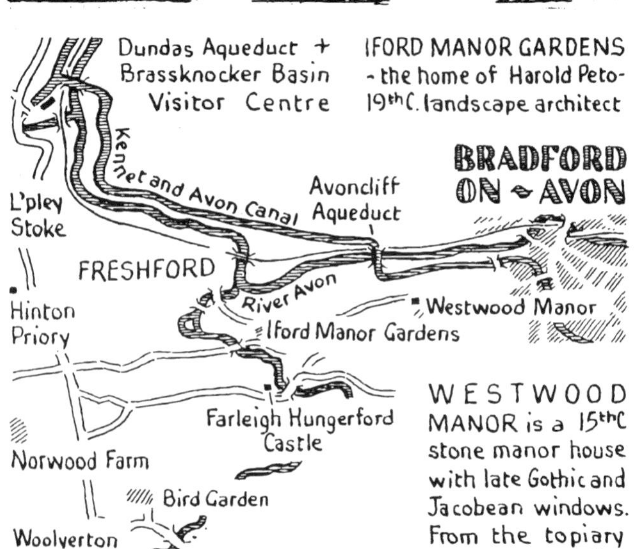

IFORD MANOR GARDENS - the home of Harold Peto - 19th C. landscape architect

AVONCLIFF AQUEDUCT positively leaps across the River Avon carrying the Kennet and Avon Canal - another monument to the genius of the 19th C. engineer. Rennie *(see Dundas)*. The tiny canalside settlement of Avoncliff contains a 17th Century Inn

WESTWOOD MANOR is a 15th C stone manor house with late Gothic and Jacobean windows. From the topiary garden there are fine views of the R. Frome

RODE BIRD GARDENS plays host to more than 200 species of exotic birds in a formal Victorian Garden, complete with a miniature railway

THE MEDIEVAL BRIDGE across the River Frome *(a tributary of the River Avon)* at Freshford was mentioned by Henry VIII's chronicler John Leland. The gabled building behind - The Inn - dates from Tudor times. Freshford was the first of many local villages to become a Conservation Area after the introduction of the Town and Country Planning Acts and in 1952 its timeless tranquility was acknowledged by Ealing Studios who filmed the village for the opening scenes of *The Titfield Thunderbolt*.

THE SEALED KNOT recreate medieval life in Farleigh Hungerford Castle, built in 1377 by Sir Thomas Hungerford, First Speaker of the House of Commons whilst his son Walter, High Treasurer of England under Henry VI, extended the Castle Southwards. Expertly preserved by English Heritage.

IN FOUR CENTURIES the Romans left more traces of their civilization in N E Somerset than is often realised, as the old Roman Road in the Hills above Freshford shows. Bath *(Aquae Sulis)* was clearly a major Roman town through which ran the Fosse Way; whilst Roman lead and silver mining in the Mendips was linked to Camerton pewter

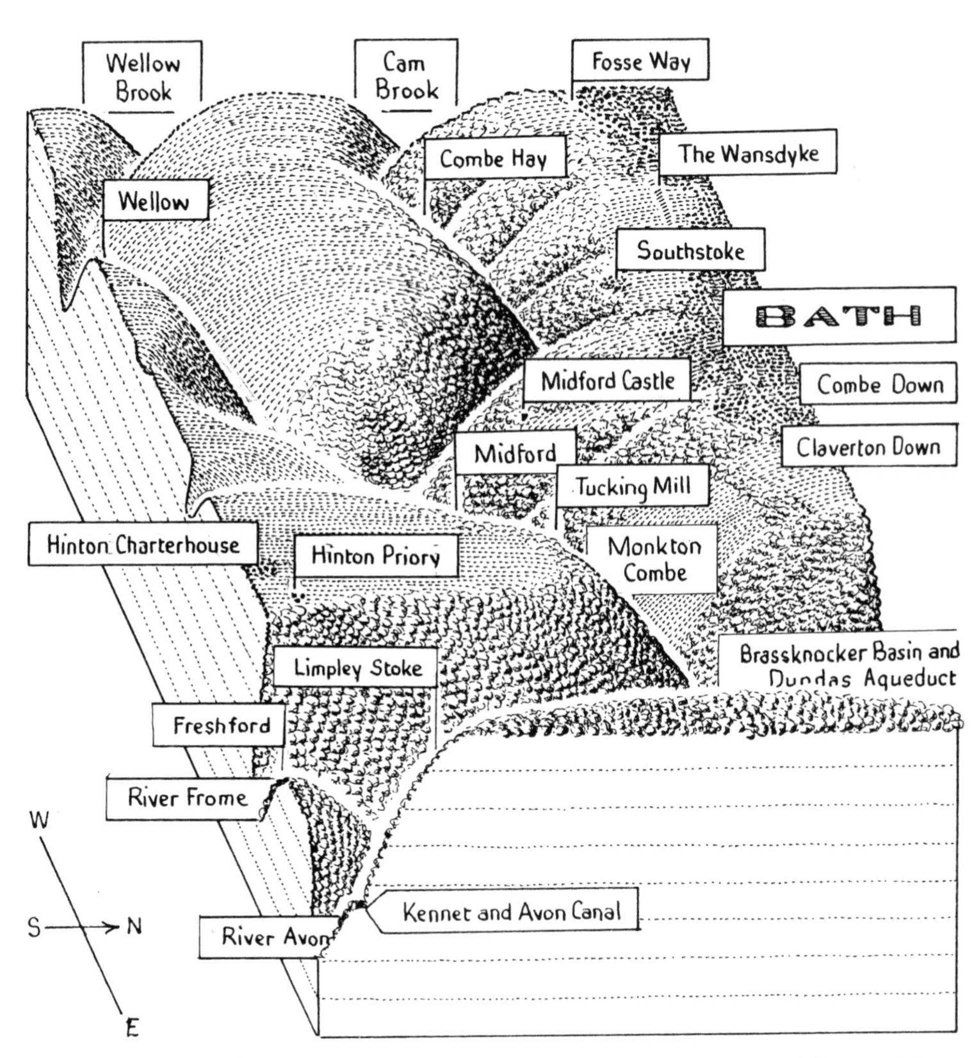

3D diagram of the complex network of valleys South of Bath where the Wellow and Cam Brooks combine to form the Midford Brook which in turn joins the River Avon near its confluence with the River Frome.

THE VALLEYS OF THE WELLOW BROOK:

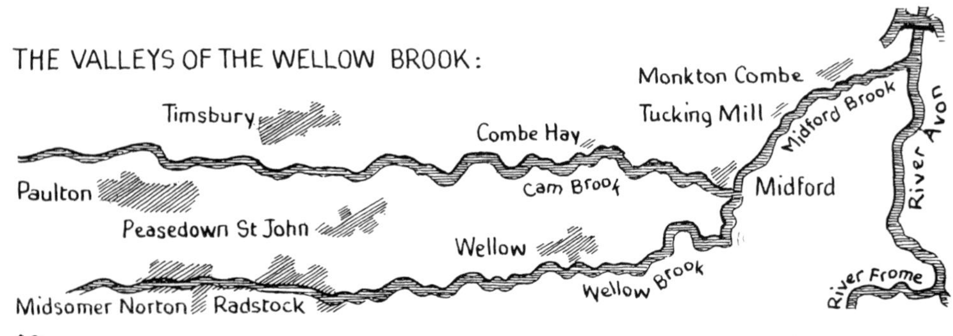

CHAPTER 3

THE VALLEYS OF THE WELLOW BROOK

ANCIENT TREES surround Somerset's oldest house : now the Old Priory Hotel and Restaurant in Church Square, Midsomer Norton, the building dates back to 1160.

"The Valleys of the Wellow Brook" are a network of rivers whose individual names change as often as the countryside through which they flow. Rising in the foothills of the Mendips in an area rich in industrial heritage ~ from long gone coalfields and rail networks ~ the various tributaries combine to form two meandering rivers ~ the Wellow and Cam Brooks. After wandering through lush green valleys scattered with such memorable olde English villages as Combe Hay and Wellow the two Brooks themselves combine to form the Midford Brook which rushes through its deeply wooded valley before joining the River Avon at Limpley Stoke.

This then is a river system not only rich in *natural* history but soaked in a wide spectrum of *physical* history too. Here, for instance, in Cameley, amongst beautiful grey stone and red tiled farms is a little red tiled Church set amongst yew trees. Sir John Betjeman described it as "Rip-Van-Winkles" Church, looking as if it had been asleep for 150 years. Most of the structure is 12th Century, the interior Jacobean and the pews are 15th Century.

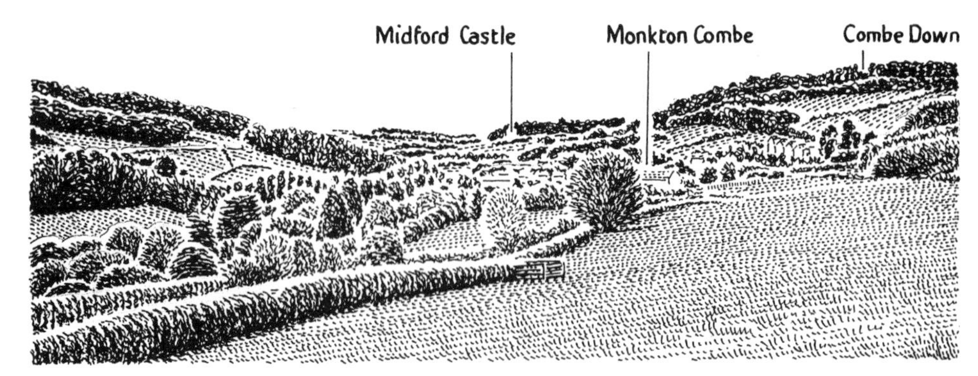

THE VALLEY OF THE MIDFORD BROOK drawn from a high point above Limpley Stoke. In the foreground lies the village of Monkton Combe, dominated by its famous public school which was founded in the 19th Century to teach the children of missionaries. In the distance Midford Castle was built in 1775 for Henry Disney Roebuck in the shape of an ace of clubs ~ apparently to commemorate Roebuck's considerable success at gambling with cards!

DEEP IN THE WOODED VALLEY of the Midford Brook lies the small hamlet of Tucking Mill; a plaque on one of the beautiful houses *(above)* reads "Here lived William Smith, father of English geology, 1769 ~ 1839". Smith, who earned the nickname "Strata Smith", pioneered the science of rock stratification and identification by their fossil content; in 1794 he was also appointed Engineer for the construction of the Somerset Coal Canal.

The Valleys of the Wellow Brook

BATH'S SECRET GARDEN

The Midford Brook and the lower reaches of the Cam Brook curl around the southern boundary of Bath hardly a stones throw from the city. Yet despite this proximity you will find here countryside as unspoiled as a national park, delightfully picturesque little villages, dense natural woodland and a web of wonderfully wild wooded walks.

THE 15th CENTURY TOWER of Combe Hay Church rises above the trees. This attractive village is rural England at its best, yet, amazingly, 200 years ago Combe Hay was the centre of activity in an attempt to solve a huge civil engineering problem. The Paulton arm of the Somersetshire Coal Canal was built at two levels, the upper level from Paulton to Combe Hay and the lower level from Combe Hay to Limpley Stoke. The steep incline at their junction was eventually navigated in 1805 by a flight of 22 locks ~ 18 of which are still visible *(although only 7 are accessible to the public)*. However, the original plan had been to build three "Caisson" locks ~ an experimental system in which each barge was raised 45ft in a large watertight box. It failed.

SOUTH STOKE is a picturesque village built mostly in Bath stone with an interesting old pub called the Packhorse Inn; no doubt packhorse drivers once relished the opportunity to quench their thirsts after leading their animals up the steep slope from Combe Hay. Legend tells of a tunnel which connected the Inn to the Church, a building largely rebuilt in 1712 although its tower is 16th Century and its North doorway is Norman.

THE DELIGHTFUL SITUATION OF MIDFORD belies its transport heritage ~ for a spaghetti of railways, canals, tramways and roads once crammed into this deep wooded valley. In 1815 Midford became the trans-shipment point for coal ~ hauled by horses down the tramway from Radstock and transfered into barges on the Somersetshire Coal Canal. The famous Somerset and Dorset Railway steamed across its 8 arch viaduct here carrying it over the Bath Road, the Cam Brook, the Somersetshire Coal Canal and the GWR Limpley Stoke to Camerton Branch Line! Midford has almost as many bridge arches as people, and the aqueduct carrying the Somersetshire Coal Canal has now been restored by the Avon Industrial Buildings Trust using a grant from the Heritage Lottery Commission.

THE GEORGE INN, NORTON ST PHILIP, must surely be one of England's most famous public houses. Built of local brown stone with jettied timber framed first and second floors, it is arguably Britain's oldest licensed premises, beginning life in 1230 as a guest house for Hinton Priory. After the dissolution of the monasteries in 1539 it became an Inn.

ELITE GUEST LIST: availing yourself of the hospitality offered by the George Inn will place you in good company. Samuel Pepys "dined very well" here for 10 shillings in 1668, whilst in 1685, when the hotel offered 35 beds and stabling for 90 horses, it played its part in the Monmouth Rebellion. The Duke of Monmouth had landed in Lyme Regis on 11 June 1685 determined to overthrow King James II; gathering an army en route he arrived at the George Inn after turning back from Bath and made it his headquarters for the night. Indeed, he is said to have been shot at while standing beside an upstairs window – Monmouth was eventually defeated at the Battle of Sedgemoor on 6 July 1685, after which "Hanging Judge Jeffreys" held some of his "bloody assizes" here.

Samuel Pepys

"Hanging Judge Jeffreys"

A GREAT CARTHUSIAN MONASTERY

The villages of Hinton Charterhouse and Norton St Philip were both possessions of Hinton Priory, England's second Carthusian Monastery founded in 1232. "Charterhouse" was the name given by Carthusian monks to their monastic settlements, whilst Norton St Philip, which then stood on the main road between Bath and Salisbury, was used as a market to sell their wool.

HINTON PRIORY was dissolved in 1539; all that remains today are the Chapter House with library and dovecote above, the undercroft of the refectory, the sacristy and parts of the guest house. Excavations in the 1950's revealed the outline of the Church and the great cloister.

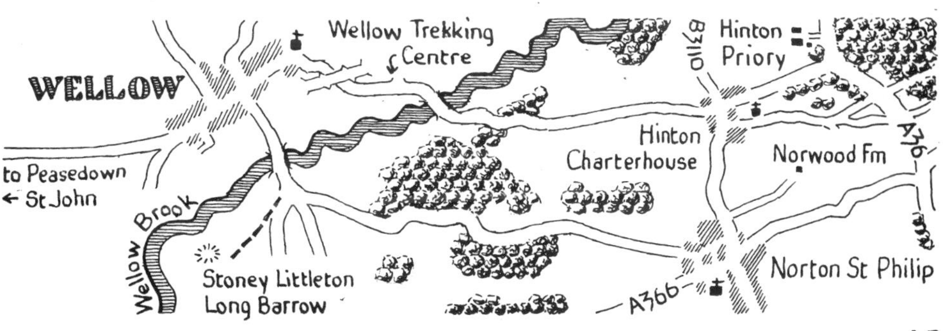

THE DOVE COTE in the grounds of the M
House would have been used to
fresh meat in medi

THE NATIONAL ANTHEM was written by John Bull who lived in Wellow

WELLOW STATION, now converted into a house, stood on the S&DJR *(see page 25)* between Midford and Shoscombe / Single Hill Halt.

THE ANCIENT AND THE NEW: a medieval packhorse bridge across the Wellow Brook overlooks a more modern ford. The house behind the bridge was once the village corn mill.

WELLOW PARISH CHURCH is 14th Century: workmen removing an old organ in 1951 rediscovered unique 15th century wall paintings of Christ and the Apostles.

PERHAPS this Neolithic Soldier guarded Stoney Littleton Long Barrow 4,000 years ago? Now one of England's finest restored prehistoric tombs, this is a chambered barrow in the style of a 10ft high wedge shaped mound with a horned forecourt. Once inside a 40ft long gallery leads to three pairs of side chambers and one at the far end.

The Valleys of the Wellow Brook

AN OLDE ENGLISH VILLAGE

Stop awhile in Wellow – an attractive little village which would not look out of place in the Cotswolds. Ancient Wellow was closely associated with the Hungerford family, whose 17th Century manor house, complete with Dovecote, faces onto the High Street. Indeed Sir Thomas Hungerford, first Speaker of the House of Commons, was the original Patron of Wellow Church when it was built in 1372. Add a welcoming pub, a medieval pack horse bridge across the Wellow Brook and even an old country railway station converted into a house and the image is complete. Well ~ almost complete ~ for in the best tradition of English villages Wellow also has a ghost, associated with St Julian's Well in the valley a little East of the Church.

WELLOW sketched from across th
from Stoney Littleton Long Barrow

HORSES AND RIDERS from the Wellow Trekking Centre canter through the village square. Behind them stands the Manor House whilst on the right *(their left)* is the Fox and Badger.

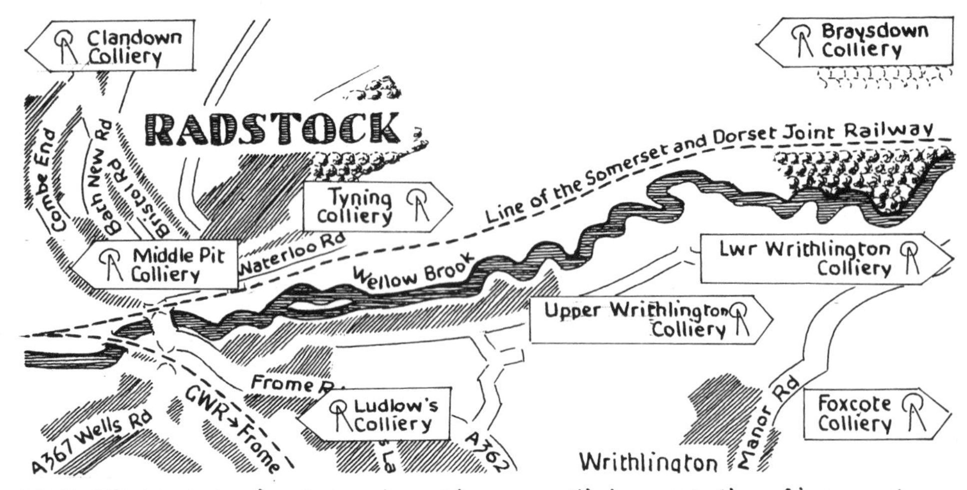

MAP of Radstock showing the locations of its many collieries and the lines of its two railways

JACK AND JILL HILL: the hill of nursery rhyme fame is reputed to lie a little South of Radstock in the village of Kilmersdon. Local legend tells that Jack suffered a fatal fall in a quarry whilst Jill died in childbirth leaving her son to be brought up by the village womenfolk. The hilltop well of Jack and Jill notoriety was renovated in 1999 ready for the millenium.

A 9F 2-10-0 engine steams out of Radstock North Station in the early 1960's, ready to tackle the arduous 7 mile, 1 in 55 ascent up to Maesbury Summit. Two railway companies forced their way into Radstock's narrow valley: the Great Western Railway (GWR) from Bristol to Frome opened in 1854 after which the Somerset and Dorset Joint Railway (S&DJR) linked Bath with the south coast in 1875. Subsequent colliery connections laid by both railway companies ensured that this valley was a 'railway spaghetti!' The two main lines ran parallel through Radstock *(see map)* giving this little town two stations and two level crossings ~ the latter used to jam Saturday afternoon cars for miles each side of the town as early as the 1950's. The S&DJR finally closed in 1966 and the GWR line in 1968, *although Radstock's GWR signal box is now used at the Didcot R/wy Centre.*

KING COAL

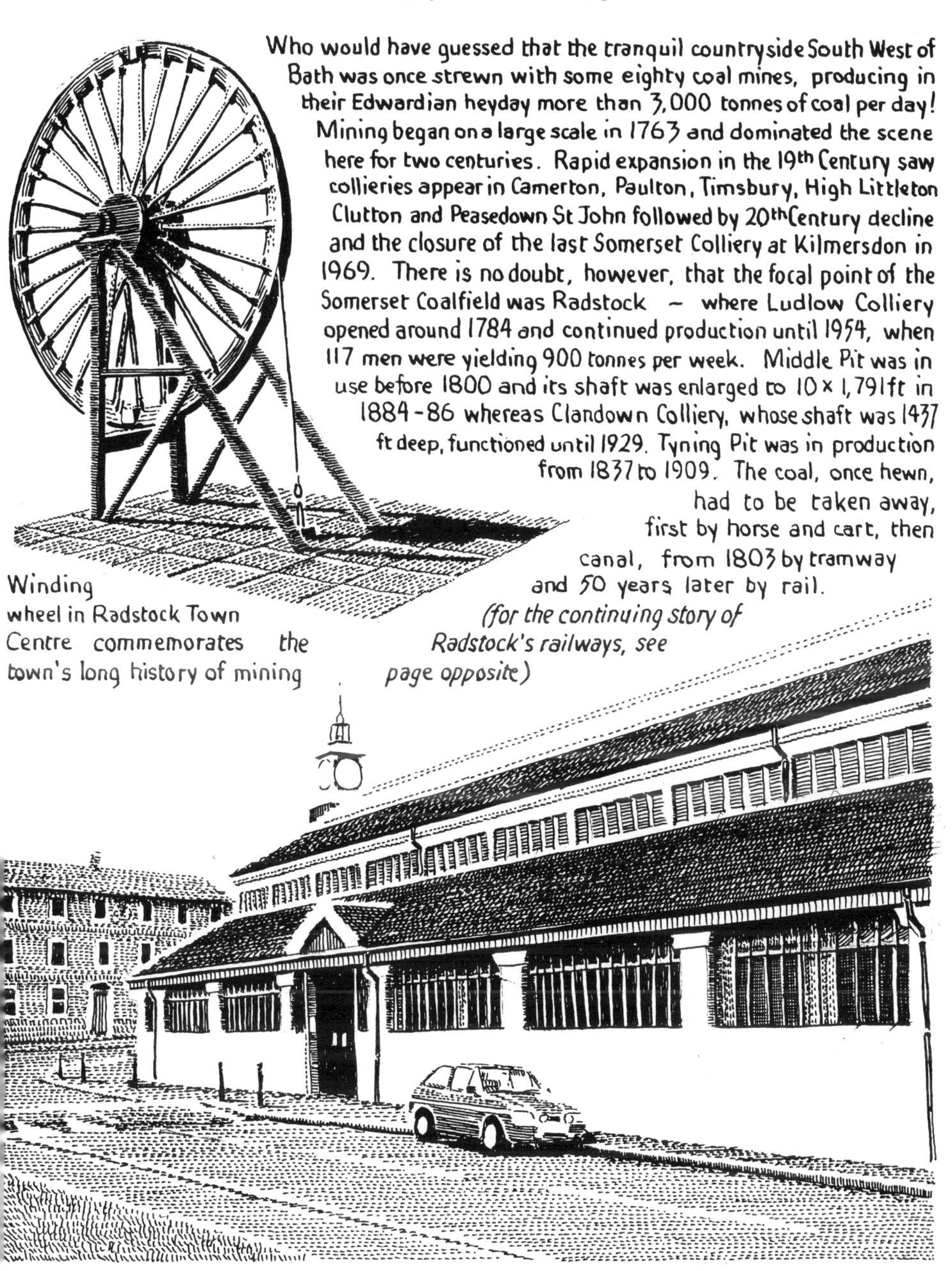

Who would have guessed that the tranquil countryside South West of Bath was once strewn with some eighty coal mines, producing in their Edwardian heyday more than 3,000 tonnes of coal per day! Mining began on a large scale in 1763 and dominated the scene here for two centuries. Rapid expansion in the 19th Century saw collieries appear in Camerton, Paulton, Timsbury, High Littleton Clutton and Peasedown St John followed by 20th Century decline and the closure of the last Somerset Colliery at Kilmersdon in 1969. There is no doubt, however, that the focal point of the Somerset Coalfield was Radstock – where Ludlow Colliery opened around 1784 and continued production until 1954, when 117 men were yielding 900 tonnes per week. Middle Pit was in use before 1800 and its shaft was enlarged to 10 × 1,791ft in 1884-86 whereas Clandown Colliery, whose shaft was 1437 ft deep, functioned until 1929. Tyning Pit was in production from 1837 to 1909. The coal, once hewn, had to be taken away, first by horse and cart, then canal, from 1803 by tramway and 50 years later by rail.

Winding wheel in Radstock Town Centre commemorates the town's long history of mining

(for the continuing story of Radstock's railways, see page opposite)

LOCAL HISTORY BROUGHT TO LIFE: Radstock Museum, recently moved to a magnificent building in the town centre, commemorates life and work in the Somerset Coalfield with a re-constructed mine tunnel, Co-op shop and schoolroom. *(+, of course, a tea shoppe)*

MIDSOMER NORTON

Just West of Radstock, where the Wellow Brook is joined by the River Somer, lies Midsomer Norton. Surprisingly, the town draws its quaint name neither from its river or, as John Wesley once suggested, its muddy 18th Century roads which allowed access only in midsummer, but because its Church is dedicated to St John the Baptist whose festival is on Midsummer's Day.

THE RIVER SOMER is neatly canalised down one side of Midsomer Norton's main street forming one of North East Somerset's most attractive town centres.

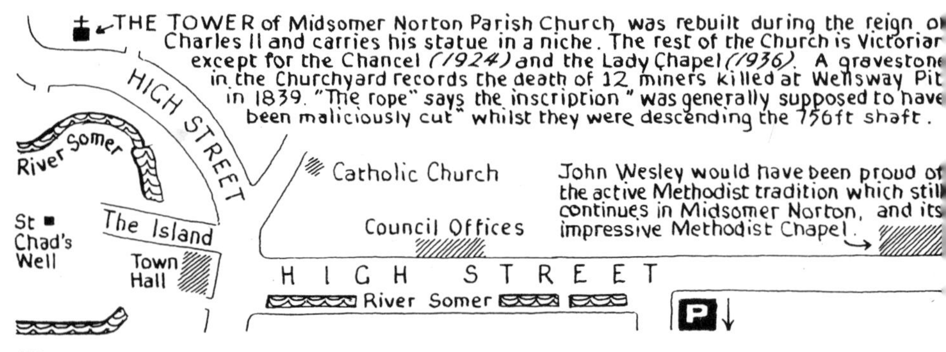

THE TOWER of Midsomer Norton Parish Church was rebuilt during the reign of Charles II and carries his statue in a niche. The rest of the Church is Victorian except for the Chancel *(1924)* and the Lady Chapel *(1936)*. A gravestone in the Churchyard records the death of 12 miners killed at Wellsway Pit in 1839. "The rope" says the inscription " was generally supposed to have been maliciously cut" whilst they were descending the 756ft shaft.

John Wesley would have been proud of the active Methodist tradition which still continues in Midsomer Norton, and its impressive Methodist Chapel.

IS THIS ITALY OR NORTH EAST SOMERSET? Large overhanging eaves give Midsomer Norton's Town Hall a wonderfully Italianate look. Built in 1860 as a Market Hall it became Town Hall in 1873 amidst much wrangling with Whitehall over funding. Behind, within a small park, St Chad's Well is marked by an obelisk; in 1979 Midsomer Norton was in uproar after the Well dried up during local water authority tunnelling work.

BARN CONVERSION: the Roman Catholic Church is one of the oldest buildings in the town, converted from a 15th Century Tithe Barn which once belonged to the Augustinian Priory in Merton, Surrey. Purchased by Downside Abbey in 1906 it was converted by Sir Gilbert Scott *(architect of the Albert Memorial, London)* and consecrated in 1913.

3D diagram of the Chew Valley rising in the Mendips and flowing down to meet the Rive
Avon in Keynsham; the view is from the North looking South.

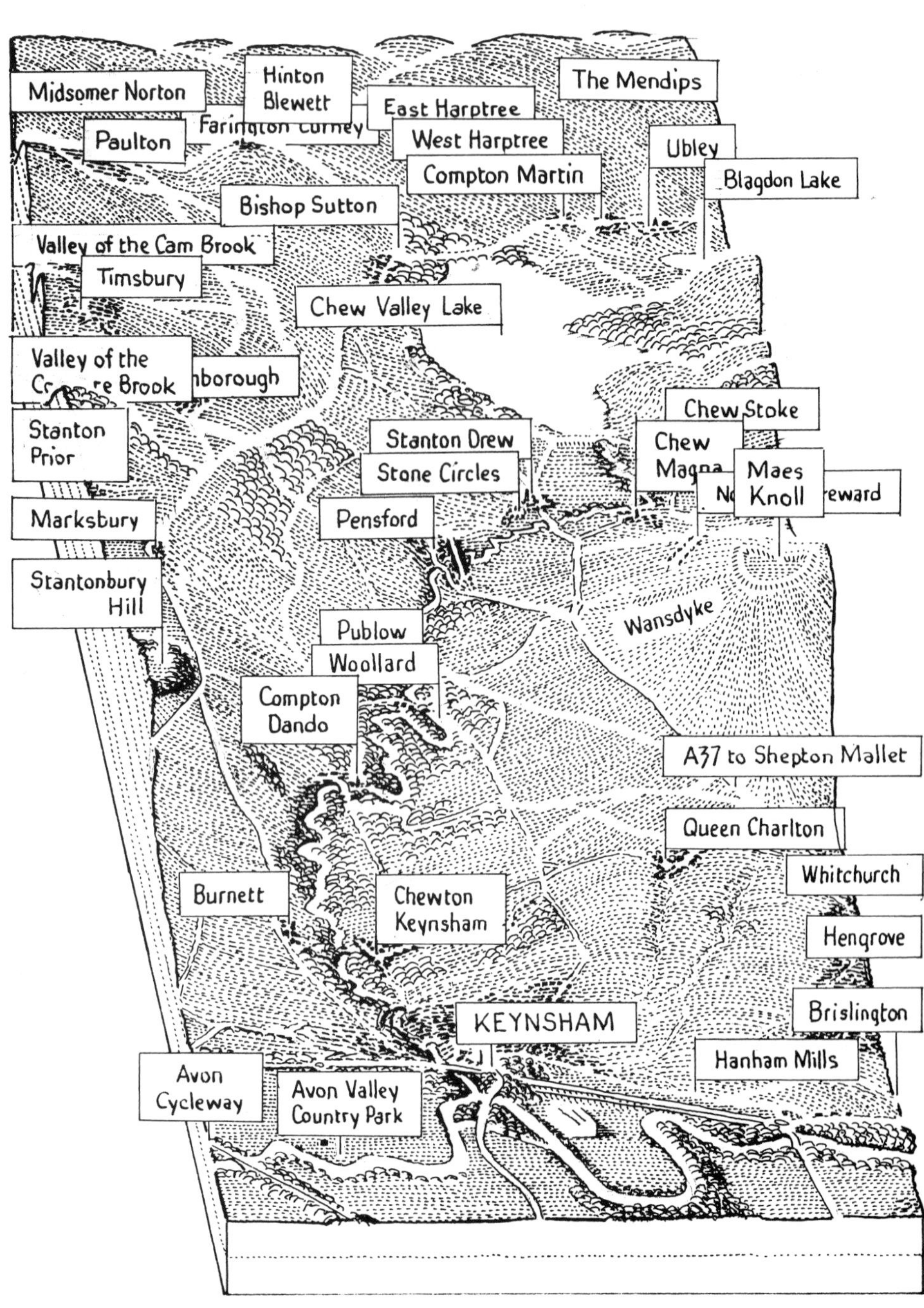

CHAPTER 4

THE CHEW VALLEY

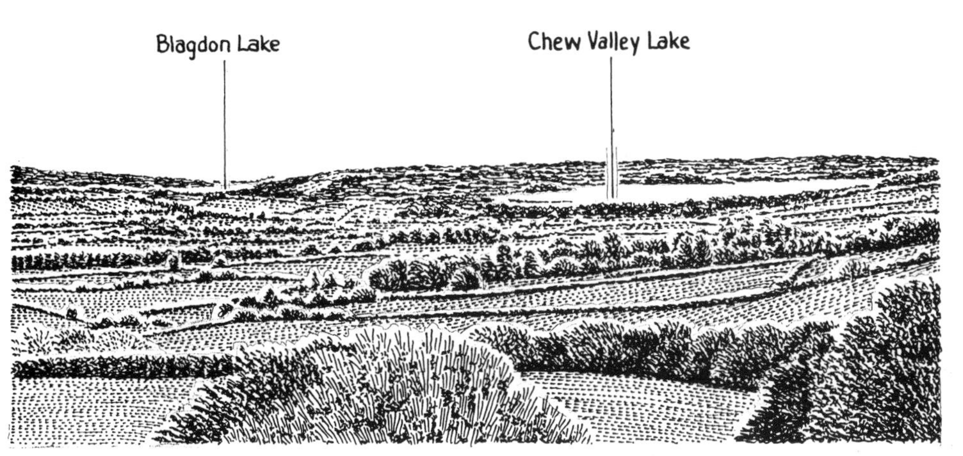

A PANORAMIC VIEW across North East Somerset's Lake District and the hills beyond drawn from Prospect Style just West of the village of Hinton Blewett.

THE RIVER CHEW rises in the foothills of the Mendips and flows into Chew Valley Lake, a large reservoir which supplies Bristol with water. After leaving the lake it flows into Chew Magna and Compton Dando, forming a fertile undulating valley before joining the River Avon at Keynsham.

The Chew Valley has a mythical air caused by such legendary sites as the Stanton Drew Stone Circles, the lost Richmont Castle and the Iron Age hill fort on the top of Maes Knoll.

THE RIVER CHEW cascades over the weir and down the trout ladder at the site of Chew Mill in Keynsham's Memorial Park. Originally a grist mill owned by Keynsham Abbey, it later became a battery mill using water powered hammers to shape brass ingots.

The Chew Valley

WALKING COUNTRY

As the tree lined River Chew meanders through the lower reaches of its valley it forms some of the most lush, gentle and picturesque walking meadows in England.

WILDLIFE HAVEN: an illustration drawn whilst walking down into the Chew Valley looking towards the hamlet of Burnett on the far ridge. Farmers in this area have agreed to preserve natural hedgerows to encourage a rich natural flora and fauna.

FAMILY WALKING: take a look at any good map of the lower Chew Valley and you will be astounded by the sheer number of footpaths which criss cross the area. Riverside walks, field walks, woodland walks and hillwalks all feature, alongside such long distance paths as the Three Peaks Circular Walk which connects Pensford, Clutton and Chew Magna. *(The three peaks involved are Maes Knoll (see next 4 pages), Blackberry Hill ~ a Lower Lias ridge near Clutton, and Knowle Hill.*

3 PEAKS

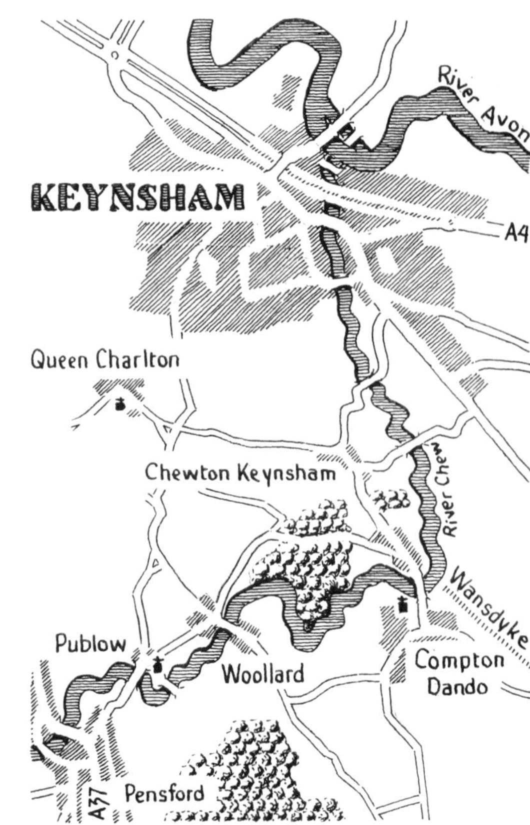

A GEM IN A BEAUTIFUL SETTING: the Somerset Perpendicular Church Tower at Publow rises above the riverside treetops,....

....AND HIDDEN BELOW THE TREES: Publow's medieval bridge over the meandering River Chew

SO THIS IS WHERE BATH'S GREAT ROMAN ALTAR WENT! The Parish Church of St Mary in Compton Dando has a piece of Roman Sculpture built into the NE buttress of the Chancel. Although badly worn, the figure is Jupiter and the stone is now recognised as a missing part of the great altar from the Roman temple in Bath. Here we also meet again the Wansdyke, believed to have been built in the 6th or 7th Century by the Ancient Britons to arrest the advance of the Saxons. Its effect, however, was only temporary; in 577AD the Saxon Kings Cuthwine *(illustrated)* and Caewlin defeated the Ancient British Kings at the Battle of Dyrham *(near Dyrham Park)* after which Somerset, Gloucestershire and Bristol all became Saxon.

Saxon King Cuthwine

HIGH PEAK

The descent from Maes Knoll looking towards Keynsham. The summit of Maes Knoll is the site of an Iron Age Hill Fort whose ramparts make the final climb to the top positively alpine. However, the reward for all the effort is a most magnificent view over the Avon Valley from Clifton to Saltford and the Chew Valley from Keynsham to the Mendips.

HIGH TOWER: Poised on top of Dundry Hill the tower of Dundry Church is one of Bristol's most famous landmarks. Indeed, that was its purpose, built in the 15th Century by the Merchant Venturers of Bristol to aid ship navigation and thus designed to be visible for many miles around. Standing nearly 100ft high the tower has the most ornate crown, with elaborate pinnacles and parapet. Of course with a landmark comes a magnificent view; Bristol seen from Dundry appears as a model, laid out at ones feet!

HORSEWORLD is a new visitor centre in Whitchurch which offers a memorable family experience of horses, ponies and donkeys.

IMPRESSIVE HEIGHT

From the windy heights of Dundry Hill and the Iron Age Hill Fort on the summit of Maes Knoll *(from where the whole Chew Valley from Keynsham to the Mendips can be seen like a green carpet at ones feet)* down to the old wool village of Pensford which suffered badly in the 1968 floods ~ one recurring theme dominates all that one sees ~ Height

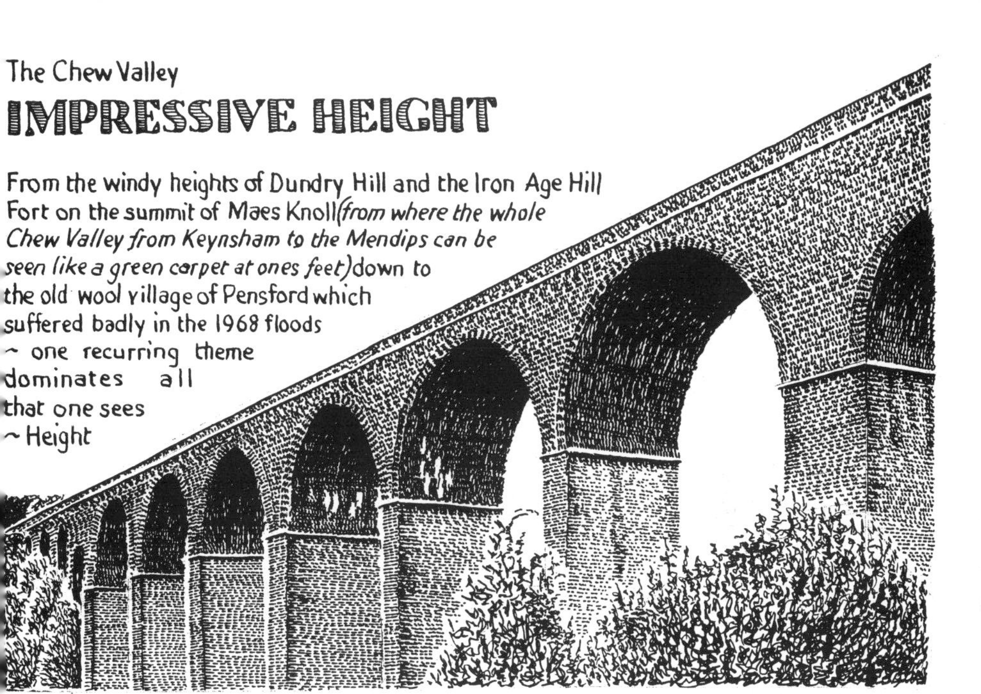

HIGH ARCHES: Pensford is dominated by the 16 arches of its massive stone and brick viaduct, built in 1873 to carry the GWR railway from Bristol to Frome. Whilst the line was closed to passengers in 1959 it remained open for freight until the flood of 1968.

HIGH WATER MARK: plaques on Church St show the flood level on 10th July 1968, which reached bedroom height.

HEIGHT OF NAUGHTINESS: the last occupant of Pensford's octagonal 18th Century lock up was a young boy caught stealing a turnip from a field. Other historic buildings in the village include 2 coaching Inns and a Tudor cottage.

MYTH AND MYSTERY

The incredible legends and folklore which surround the neolithic Stone Circles in Stanton Drew are more romantic ~ but no more amazing ~ than archaeological views of their origin.

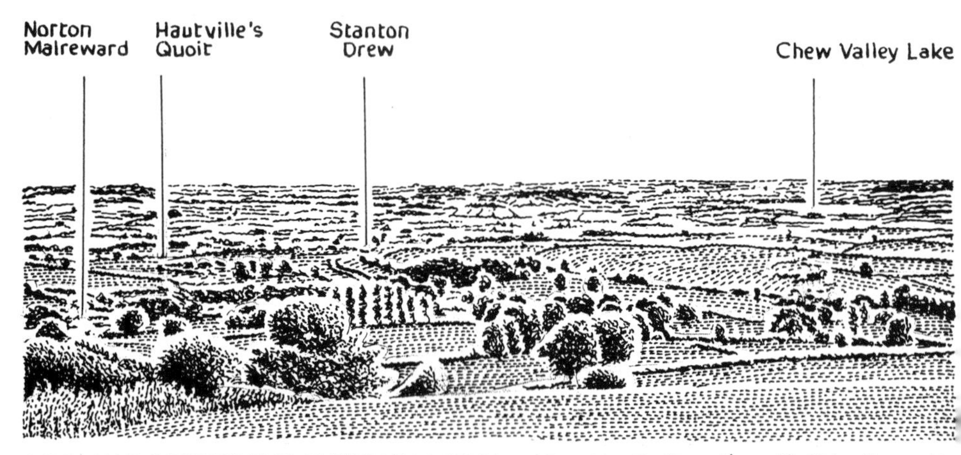

LOOKING ACROSS THE CHEW VALLEY from Maes Knoll. From here Sir John Hautville is said to have thrown in anger a 30 tonne stone now known as "Hautville's Quoit".

OF GIANTS AND INCREDIBLE FEATS: A wooden effigy of Sir John Hautville lies uncomfortably in Chew Magna Church. Romantic legend tells that Sir John, who lived in Norton Hawkfield, was a giant who impressed King Edward I with his great strength. The King rewarded Sir John by giving him lands in the parish, but our hero was unimpressed. In disgust he renamed the parish Norton "*Mal-reward*" then climbed to the top of Maes Knoll and hurled a huge stone from the summit. It landed in a field north of Stanton Drew and is known today as "Hautville's Quoit" ~ although there seems little doubt that the Quoit is actually part of the Stanton Drew Stone Circles.

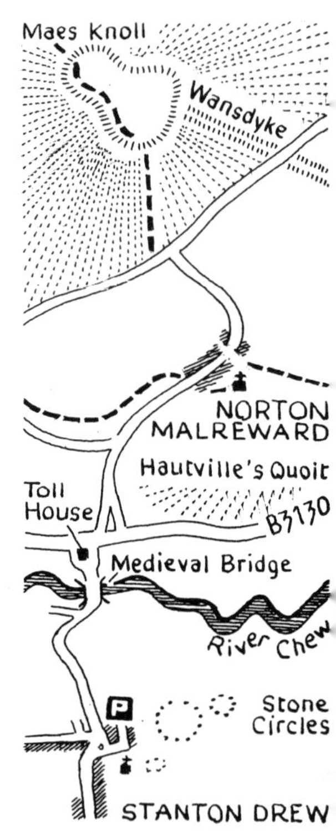

LOOKING BACK TO THE FUTURE: looking towards the Iron Age Hill Fort on top of Maes Knoll from a monolith at Stanton Drew. Although both are prehistoric sites, the Stanton Drew stones had already stood for 1,000 years before the camp at the summit of Maes Knoll was built.

THE STONE CIRCLES at Stanton Drew have attracted many traditions to explain their origin, the most famous of which tells that the stones were a wedding party intent on dancing through Saturday evening into the Sabbath. At midnight the piper refused to play on and the irate bride threatened to find another one from hell, but the celebrations were saved by a mysterious piper who arrived and offered to play. As they continued to dance the music grew faster and faster and the dancers were unable to stop, realising too late that the new piper was the devil himself. When the music stopped they were all turned to stone.

Another legend predicts the same fate if anyone counts or draws the stones....

THE NORTH EAST CIRCLE at Stanton Drew; one can see a piper and dancers at its centre

STANTON DREW has three large stone circles, of which the largest 'Great' Circle is 360ft diameter and has 27 of its original 30 stones still standing. Adjacent to the 'Great Circle' is the smallest 'North East' Circle with just 8 stones. Near the Church the 'South West' Circle has twelve stones. In the grounds of the local pub *(a great excuse to visit this friendly establishment!)* three stones form "The Cove" which may have been a burial chamber. All the stones are believed to be part of a complex Neolithic site of pagan worship contemporary with Stonehenge and Avebury.

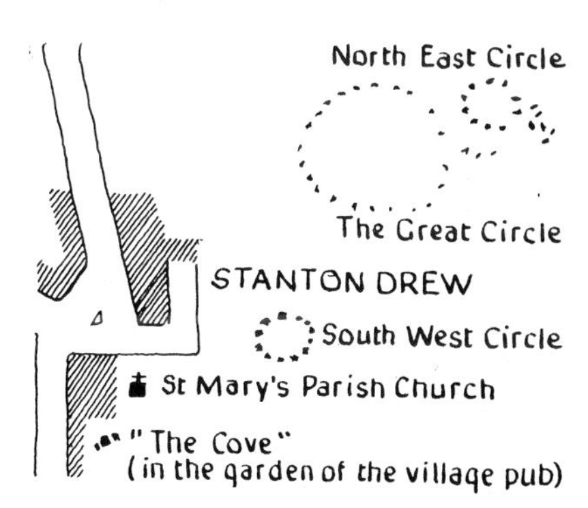

LAKESIDE VENUE: Chew Valley Lake Visitor Centre and Nature Trail drawn from the da

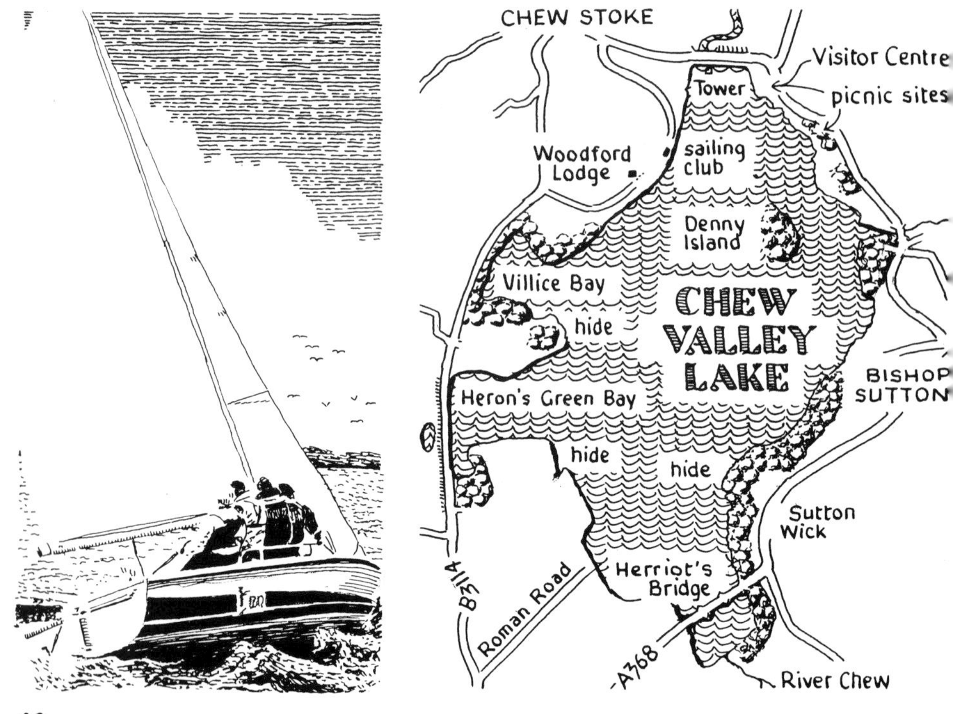

CHEW VALLEY LAKE

Completed in 1956, Chew Valley Lake covers an area of 1,200 acres *(456 ha)* and is 2½ miles long by 1½ miles wide. Although its primary purpose is to supply Bristol with water, it also provides a thriving leisure facility for sailors, fishermen, ornithologists and picnickers.......

ECOLOGY OF THE WATERLINE: most of Chew Valley Lake's 8 mile perimeter is naturally vegetated: rough grass and reed beds intersperse with larch and conifer plantations whilst Denny Island is covered with mature deciduous trees. The only evidence of mans intervention is the dam at the Northern end and several road causeways, although the additional shelter the causeways create yields a specially rich flora and fauna.

ORNITHOLOGISTS PARADISE: Chew Valley Lake is one of Britains most important wildfowl sites, currently home to more than 250 different species. Amongst the surface feeders Mallard, Wigeon, and Teal dominate whilst Pochard, Tufted Ducks, Goldeneyes and Goosanders represent the divers. Gulls are here in their thousands, roosting here as do the Coots and the Mute Swans. In the reed beds you may see Grey Heron, standing motionless ready to ambush the next fish which dares to swim near, whilst Buzzards are frequently to be seen soaring over the nearby fields. The thriving Reed Warbler colony attracts parasitic Cuckoos, whilst other successful immigrants, this time from North America - Canada Geese and Ruddy Ducks - now breed here. In the latter case Chew Valley Lake is home to half the UK population.

Coot

Heron

Canada Goose

THE GREAT 15th CENTURY TOWER of St Andrews Church, almost 100ft high, dominates Chew Magna.

CHEW MAGNA *(left)* is so called because it was once the most important village on the River Chew. In the 16th Century Leland called it a "*prety cloathing townelet*" and indeed its past prosperity is reflected in its fine old buildings built above raised pavements. Chew Court, next to the Church, was once the Palace of the Bishops of Bath and Wells and was a particular favourite of Bishop John Clerk *(died 1541)* who built Horton Court in South Gloucestershire. Ton Bridge is late 15th Century and has a "well" on top of one of the buttresses; which was used when small pox was rife in the village. Farmers brought goods to the bridge and collected cash from the disinfectant filled well.

CHURCH, INN AND FARMHOUSE form a picturesque view of East Harptree, an unspoilt grey stone village and conservation area climbing the Northern slopes of the Mendip Hills.

TRANQUIL LAKESIDE VILLAGES

Surrounding the Chew Valley Lake are a series of attractive villages with delightfully peculiar names: Nempnet Thrubwell, Ubley, the Harptrees, Chew Magna, Hinton Blewett and Compton Martin. All are quiet unspoilt communities with ancient Churches and welcoming pubs, generally untroubled by the pace of modern life. Some, such as Stowey, are mere hamlets with a 13th Century Church; in its chancel are biblical murals painted by Henry Strachey in 1915 using local people as models. Other villages have existed since Roman times; Pagan Hill above Chew Stoke was once topped by an octagonal Roman temple.

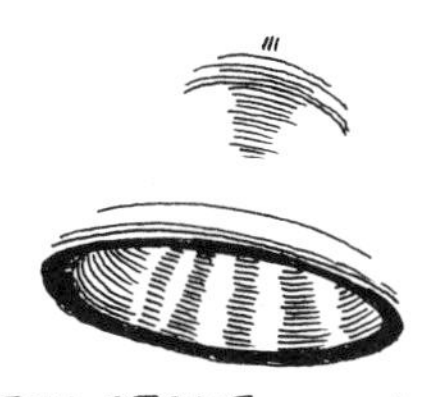

CHEW STOKE was the 18th c home of the Bilbie family, famous bell founders whose work still peals over a wide area of North East Somerset, and who decried their competitors and advertised their own skill in poetic inscriptions on their bells.

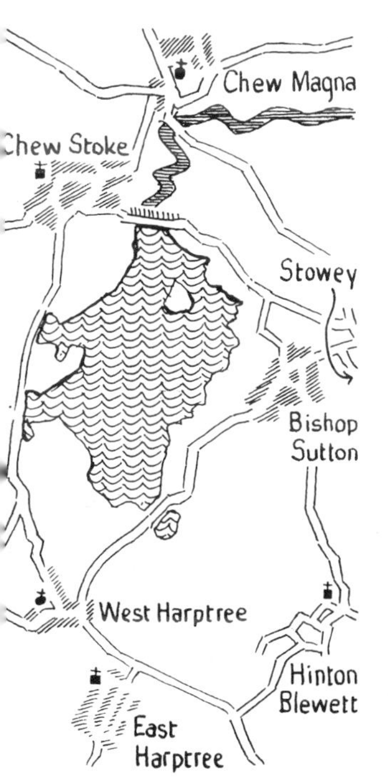

ASPIRING TO THE HEAVENS: the Church of St Mary in West Harptree was rebuilt in 1865 but retained its Norman tower, to which was added a spire. West Harptree village centre contains some spectacular 17th Century buildings such as Gournay Court and the Tilley Manor adjoining and opposite the Church. The 18th Century village Corn Mill ~ last used during the 1939 ~ 45 war - stood on land needed for the Chew Valley Reservoir and would have been destroyed, but was happily removed and rebuilt with its original machinery on the Hazel Brook in the grounds of Blaise Castle, Bristol.

THE PEACEFUL MILL POND in Compton Martin with village Post Office behind. By a happy accident, Compton Martin Parish Church contains some of the best preserved Norman architecture in Europe. 14th Century rebuilders working on the Chancel arch found to their alarm that it was starting to sink so decided to leave much of the Norman work alone. Today this settlement is clearly visible. In the 12th Century Compton Martin was the birth-place of Sir Wulfric of Haselbury, a prophet who foresaw the accession to the throne of King Stephen.

ONLY THE TELEPHONE BOX gives away that this view of Ubley Village Green is not 13th Century, and perhaps also the "Best Kept Village" plaques on the side of the restored 13th Century village cross. The 13th Century Church, which contains a chained copy of the Paraphrase of the Gospels by Erasmus of 1552 and a Jacobean wooden pulpit, is dedicated to St Bartholomew on whose feast day the right to hold an annual fair was granted in the reign of Edward II.